DOUBLE YOUR ACCOUNTING FIRM

Lessons Learned on How Top Firms Grow Faster, Build Stronger Teams, and Increase Profit While Working Less

David Cristello & Joe Cassandra

ISBN: 978-152181413-0

Complimentary Gift: Access All the Growing Your Firm Interviews for Free.

Visit Jetpackworkflow.com/interviews

Table of Contents

About the Authors

David Cristello

David Cristello the Founder & CEO Jetpack Workflow (https://jetpackworkflow.com/), a leading workflow & Recurring Client Management (RCM) Software for Accounting Firms. Jetpack was developed after seeing the amount lost work and clients deadlines falling through the cracks because of faulty processes, redundant spreadsheets, or legacy based applications. It started as a side project and now has turned into a global solution for firms all over the world. Jetpack serves thousands of accountants in 15+ countries. He works alongside the best team on the planet, and feels fortunate to be on the journey with them.

David is also the creator and host of Growing Your Firm Podcast (https://jetpackworkflow.com/category/growing-your-firm-podcast/), one of the top accounting podcasts on the planet. Each week he interviews firm leaders and experts on how to double, triple, or 10x their firm. It's all free, and has over 100,000 downloads.

Joe Cassandra

I met David after interviewing him a few years ago on my own podcast I had done. My background is in accounting before moving into writing sales copy and marketing. I work with financial companies and firms on getting more clients in the door with their marketing efforts. Clients include: Inc. 5000 companies, Business Insider, multi-million dollar financial publishers and more.

"Hiring Joe was the best decision I ever agreed to."
— Joshua, client

"Joe has proven to be a valuable asset to our organization with his stellar ability to construct discussion driving content for our marketing efforts. Our conversions have increased 25% since hiring him."
— Josh, client

To my loving wife, Rosa. I love the journey we are taking together. I'm glad it's with you.

– David

To my beautiful wife Sam and daughter Chloe. You're my favorite part of the day.

– Joe

Introduction

Dear Ambitious Owner,

By now you've likely heard the phrase, *"Work on your business, not just IN it,"* a few dozen times. You've made an effort, but the problems still linger...

- Where do I find the time, space, or energy to work "on" my business?
- How do others work on their business?

Owners and partners in accounting firms face an ever-changing landscape in the industry—there are new ways to market and sell, a younger generation of CPAs entering your firm, and ever-expanding technology. It can be overwhelming for firm owners who are used to doing things how they always have.

The truth is: the dawn of the internet has shifted clients' values and transformed the fields of marketing and sales. On top of that, we've seen more technological advances in the past 20 years than in the past 1,000. The world runs at a much faster clip than when you first opened your doors.

Your responsibility, as head of your firm, is to continually grow and increase profits, but you shoulder that pressure while struggling to keep up with constant change.

It's our hope that this book gives you a glimpse at how other accounting firm owners are doubling their businesses and bringing it into the future, without all the noise, glitz, and glamor mainstream media wants us to buy into. There is no overnight success. These owners have worked extremely hard to build a practice of their dreams and some have gone on to help other owners do the same.

Owners and partners need to be able to prospect for business to build up the firm for the next generation of leaders. They must also be able to put the right people in place to keep processes running smoothly and ensure clients stay happy. A firm of the future no longer banks on just churning out tax returns and billable hours; those firms struggle. Instead, you must bring more to the table for your clients.

To do so, you'll need to start from the foundation and build upward.

We're not here to promote a single individual, tactic, or strategy. Instead, we want to infuse a high-performance mindset into your everyday life. You can choose the path that is best suited for you, your team, your clients, your community, and your family.

Our goal is to help you avoid problems and overcome the common pitfalls that come with running a practice, such as:

- Not having the right workflow and processes to open up capacity for larger, better clients.
- Building a firm based on what you think is "normal" instead of what your clients value.
- Trying to compete on price or metaphorically "shout at the top of the mountain" to get clients.
- Having the only source of new business by word of mouth or hit-or-miss referrals.
- Blaming the market, location, competitors, or anyone else instead of taking consistent action to build a better practice.
- Leaving money on the table by not having highly profitable, complementary services and products.

And so many more.

At this point, you might be asking *"What qualifies these guys to write this book?"* Well, let me tell you.

David Cristello, Founder of Jetpack Workflow (https://jetpackworkflow.com/), serves thousands of accounting professionals globally.

His company began as a small startup, helping firms improve their workflow with modern-day technology. Now, Jetpack continues to expand globally (and has a footprint in 15+ countries).

Joe Cassandra, an accountant for years with a degree in the subject, left the technical side of accounting to build his company, JC Copy (http://jc-copy.com/), which is a marketing firm for financial firms that helps them increase their client base. His clients include many *Inc. 5000* companies, *Business Insider*, and a variety of global financial publishers.

Together, we also run the Growing Your Firm Podcast (https://jetpackworkflow.com/category/growing-your-firm-podcast/), which is a weekly show where we interview top accounting practitioners, owners, and thought leaders about what they're doing to grow their firms. This isn't an academic exercise…we're talking with actual owners on what's working NOW. Not five, 10, or 50 years ago. We humbly believe this collection of interviews, which are all free, is the single best resource for growing your firm and doubling it.

This books is broken in eight "pillars," all of which are built upon the interviews we've conducted at the Growing Your Firm Podcast (https://jetpackworkflow.com/category/growing-your-firm-podcast/). The chapters highlight these strategies in a deeper format, and provide additional resources, like relevant interviews, articles, and books, as well as exercise questions and suggested actions for moving forward.

To listen to any or all of the interviews referred to in this book, visit URL jetpackworkflow.com/interviews

Having said that, here's what's in store for you:

Chapter 1 will focus on your workflow foundation. We are clearly biased on this issue, but we do still truly believe that your firm is not fit to grow unless you have your workflow in order. Adding more clients or team members to a broken system does not fix the system! In fact, it only dries up profits, increases stress, and stagnates growth. In this chapter, we shoot you the straightforward, no BS approach to improving your workflow to open up capacity.

Chapter 2 focuses on your pricing strategy and highlights the alternative fixed- and value-based approaches that are currently used in the market. Pricing strategies and pricing optimization can become a huge component of increasing profits. You can even *decrease* your client headcount and still maintain the same revenues. We place pricing earlier in the book because improving or reviewing your price can be critical. We recommend pairing this chapter with a thorough analysis of your marketing blueprint and finding your ideal client in Chapters 3, 4, and 5.

Chapter 3 is to designed to help you build out your marketing blueprint. Now that you have your workflow, pricing, and foundational clients in place, you can begin to build the system that is going to generate new clients, month in and month out. If you do not have a system in place, your firm will constantly face problems with cash flow—some months will be great and others will be slow, so you can't predictably scale your business. If you want to hire new staff and scale your firm, you need a predictable marketing system.

Chapter 4 will be a crash course in how you can sell and close at a faster rate. Most accountants do not enjoy the "hard sell." We will show you how to sell like an expert without being the snake-oil car salesmen we all fear. We provide the scripts and tactics you can use.

Chapter 5 is about finding your ideal client and building out systematic, smart referral systems. Now, be warned: do NOT skip over the content on finding the ideal client. We all love the latest social media tactic or cold calling, but when you use only these tactics, you will dramatically underperform those who nail their ideal customer. We're going to focus on helping you build your foundation here, and then layer in smart referral tactics you can use to consistently bring in more clients like them.

Chapter 6 covers building and retaining your team. This is, by far, one of the most common pain points we hear about with firms that are growing. In this section, we cover the exact tactics smart owners are using to both attract and retain their top talent. The future of your firm will come from the team members you bring in. Your culture is more important than ever with the younger generation, so we include ideas you can tap into and implement to make improvements right now.

Chapter 7 focuses on building additional revenue sources. We intentionally cover this at the end because it's a "nice to have," not a "must" for today's firms. However, for those that do have a foundation in place, adding profit centers is a great way to gain market dominance, increase profits, and create ultimate expert positioning. Again, this is not the first, second, or fifth step. Thinking of new profit centers only comes into play once you're running a highly profitable firm.

Chapter 8: We included an eighth pillar as more of a bonus chapter, which is based on information we've gathered on the FASTEST way to double your firm virtually overnight. This pillar centers around mergers and acquisitions. We've had an owner show us how to acquire competition without any of the risk.

David Cristello & Joe Cassandra

One Thing to Remember

Building a business, any business, can be challenging. There are going to be days when you feel like nothing is working, or that your business will not survive. If you get nothing else from this book, just remember to *keep going*.

Keep learning, keep serving, and keep investing in yourself, your team, and your business. With consistent action, you *can* build the firm of your dreams. The difference between yours and massively successful ones is that they have already implemented these strategies, consistently and diligently, over years. Not days, not weeks, or months, but *years*. Be consistent, keep taking action, and never stop learning and growing.

With that in mind, let's dive in.

Chapter 1

Increasing your Workflow Efficiency to Increase Capacity

Sam started his practice ten years ago. He worked "typical" 80-hour weeks to build his dream firm. He hired a dozen workers spread out between CPA practitioners and administrative staff. His firm grew and referrals came through the door. That's when the cracks started to form.

Deadlines were missed. Client documents disappeared. Hours increased. Staff was burned out. Clients became upset and left.

But what was even more surprising was the amount of stress this growth would cause for Sam. Growth was supposed to be good. No longer did running a firm feel *cool*. It was now causing him to stay awake at night thinking, *"Did I miss a deadline?"* or *"Did I forget that client request?"* His firm, which seemed so simple just six months ago, was out of control.

This is what happens as your firm grows, and you encounter the fortunate problem of workflow management (even though it's a "fortunate problem", doesn't mean it's painless to solve!)

I get it. When you start off, you are simply trying to make things work, so a bit of duct tape here, a quick clean-up there, and you get by. But, if you're trying to double, triple or multiply the size of your firm, the house of duct tape will fall fast. Capacity will get squeezed, your employees will see increasing hours with little return, and clients will see deadlines come and go.

This is what happens when you don't have the right workflow systems in place. Capacity gets stretched when it could've been avoided.

You might see this in your firm right now. If you need a check, look back at the past six months and find out how many deadlines you hit and how many you missed.

Next, get a barometer check of your employees. What's the mood like in meetings? Have you seen a shift in morale? Are employees working more and more?

If you're struggling with capacity and workflow efficiency, I would guess you are still running your firm on the "billable hour." I'll touch on this in Chapter 2, but running your firm based on *time* will make your team inefficient as you aren't focused on the *result* (Note: Billable hour is still OK under many circumstances, but you must focus on the result you're trying to achieve).

It's easy to look back and see the mistakes. You might wonder how it got to this point. Sam certainly did.

Many firms end up in this predicament at some point or another. It might be at 12 employees; it might be at 5, 50, or 100. Eventually, there will be a break and the reason is simple. I'll show you with an example:

Have you ever played the game "telephone"? If you remember, one person in the group would have a message that they would whisper in the ear of the person next to them. The listener then whispered to the next person, and so on. At the end, the last person to hear the message would say it out loud. Normally, giggles would break out as the final phrase was silly and significantly different than the original message.

This childhood game happens with the workflow in your firm. Sam taught his process to his first CPA hire. That CPA then trained the next one, but probably tweaked the process a bit to suit her style. Soon, after 10 iterations, none of the CPAs were doing the process the same way.

Suddenly, there are corrections going back and forth and disagreements about how the process was supposed to go. Time is wasted and clients are upset. As new clients come in the door, there aren't enough hours in the day to help them because of these inefficiencies.

How does the owner cope with new clients?

They do the obvious: they hire more and more staff and say, *"Look at us, we are growing!"* But it's a false celebration; hiring 10 people to do the work of five only sucks up more profit and decreases bonuses, while the owner has the delusion that the problem is solved.

That is, until the next wave of clients come in and capacity is overflowing and more hires are needed. Adding more bodies to a broken system *will not* solve the problem. It's just duct tape.

This was Sam's problem. I've interviewed thousands of firm owners on my podcast and found that this isn't a unique situation; it's actually fairly common.

But it should still worry you. You might feel a tiny amount of stress right now, but you are in the calm before the storm. If you don't fix this fast, you could have legacy clients packing up and moving on. That's the reality.

Now, look at the opposite end—when you get the right systems in place, you'll suddenly see you have more time and more profits at the end of the year. You will have more time because you will be automating and outsourcing more tasks. You'll pay a small price, but save hundreds of hours.

Trust me, the small fee you pay will be much less than what you pay in salaries, bonuses, and insurance for new and unnecessary CPAs.

You'll have more profits because you are hiring only the right number of people. With all your additional time and efficiency, capacity will open up fast to make room for growth. More profits means more compensation for your current staff, which keeps them on your team. CPA recruiting is a growing, cut-throat industry. Cementing your core team for the future is essential to a budding firm.

You'll also see more revenues. As capacity grows, new clients can come in and fill in the gaps. Thus, it becomes pure profit going into your pocket as you won't have to hire new people every time bundles of clients come in. And even with more clients, you'll have less stress. You won't be waking up worrying about a deadline or if you missed something. Everything gets taken care of because your workflow *works*.

In this chapter, you will learn what the best in the business do to make workflow run as efficiently as possible. Plus, I'll tell you how to increase capacity without hiring more staff.

Stress down, profits up!

Making Workflow Work

Conceptually, workflow is the high-level overview of *how work gets done*. For reference, the process you create refers to *what to do*. When you get a handle on workflow and build a process that services that workflow, efficiency goes up and you're in better shape to expand.

As you build out your workflow, keep in mind that your product *is* your workflow and the process you use to complete projects. Want to build a more profitable, scalable, referable "product"? Then dig in.

Also keep in mind that a well-functioning workflow system can take the place of a significant amount of admin staff, so putting the foundation in place can literally add thousands of dollars per person, per month to your firm.

Jeff Borcshowa, the innovator behind DreamPractice, stresses that you must have an "assembly line" process. Everything goes through the same way and comes out the same way.

"If you don't have a system in place, how can you trust your staff?" Jeff asks.

Starting at the Top

Problems occur because roles in the firm get mixed up, so let's start with a breakdown the roles in your firm.

Owners / Partners:

Normally, partners have worked in the industry for many years and are experts in their field. Hourly rates are normally over $200. Generally, a partner should be focusing on three core areas:

- Business development
- High-level, high ROI client work
- Team-building

According to Rob Nixon, international speaker, CEO of Panalitix and CPA advisor, it should be broken down like this:

- 60% Business development
- 30% Client work
- 10% Team-building

Obviously, this is going to be balanced differently for different firms. A partner heading up Compliance and Audit will probably swing more time to client work, rather than business development. That's going to happen. The point is, owners/partners are doing high ROI activities. Everything else should be delegated to the next level down.

Managers:

Managers are responsible for correctly implementing the systems passed down from the partners. Managers must discover the small cracks before they become big ones and approach owners and partners to alert.

Managers focus on:

- Client work
- Onboarding clients efficiently
- Training the system
- Team-building

Managers will normally bill between $125–$250 per hour. The majority of their time should be spent onboarding clients correctly, completing client work, and making sure the system runs smoothly.

Client work should be more of a review and not preparation. Their main objective, contrary to popular belief, is not to get client work done, but to make sure the system is moving and capacity is evenly spread out.

When a manager gets too involved in the weeds, they lose sight of their main objective and that's when the cracks start. Like partners, managers should be delegating the bulk of client work to the next level down.

Practitioners:

These are the foot soldiers. The ones taking a box of client receipts and turning it into a tax return. Much of the time, they will also be the voice of the firm for the smaller clients—remember, partners will be doing high-level work with "valuable" clients.

Most new clients should go from the onboarding manager directly into the lap of a practitioner.

A practitioner focuses on:

- Quality client work preparation
- Touchpoints with clients

Touchpoints are quick check-ins with clients to make sure your firm is top of mind, but also to plan ahead for what's going on in a client's business. Everything else is delegated down.

Practitioners normally charge $60–$120 per hour.

Administrative Staff:

Administrative staff typically don't charge for their time. They handle all the paperwork and make sure everything gets sent out to clients.

Their duties include:

- Handling paperwork
- Sending out completed work and information to clients
- Scanning

- Scheduling
- Answering phones

Administrative staff take care of the administrative work so that practitioners, managers, and partners can focus on their billable hours' work.

Can you see where there might be issues?

Notice that at the top three positions, staff are *not* involved in any administrative tasks. None of these levels should be spending non-billable time doing non-revenue producing tasks. Partners should not be scanning in documents or sorting through client paperwork. Managers shouldn't be running around trying to get all the pieces together for a project.

Hiring more administrative staff is usually what many firms don't do. They pile all the work on a few receptionists and the rest gets pushed up to the practitioners.

An admin salary is normally around $40,000. A CPA's salary starts at $50,000 and goes up from there, so you can see that it makes much more sense, not just for the workflow, but for salaries' sake, to prefer hiring administrative staff than CPAs to do administrative work.

If you save a CPA just 200 hours a year from administrative tasks, at a base rate of $100 per hour, that's $20,000 in additional revenues into the firm. If you have 5 CPAs, now you've added $100,000 in revenue. So, hiring an admin for $40,000 makes much more sense.

Now, we know where problems can occur, let's find out where you need to focus your attention.

Setting the Baseline

"What you can't measure, you can't manage"

—Peter Drucker, renowned
author and businessman

When I interview top practitioners, I ask them which metrics they track to run a successful firm. Here's what I hear all the time:

- Turnaround time on work
- Capacity and utilization
- Profit per client

In other words, successful companies know exactly how fast and efficiently they are completing work, if anyone is under- or over-utilized, and how healthy their margins are.

While workflow intertwines through all metrics, let's going to focus on turnaround time and capacity.

Turnaround Time

Turnaround time helps you understand the internal deadline for the job so you can properly schedule team members, and therefore drive a profitable job to completion.

For those not familiar with turnaround time, simply put, it's answering the question, "How many days should this take?"

Decreasing turnaround time gives your clients the best experience possible. You might not believe your clients care when you give them their work, but they do value it. Think back to this: when the pressure was on to get returns and work out the door because of the tax deadline, did it get done? Most likely, yes.

You would be surprised how efficient CPAs become when there is a deadline knocking. It actually has a name: Parkinson's Law.

What it means is that time expands to the extent work needs to be done. Meaning, if you set a realistic deadline for something to be done, as long as the focus is on that task, it will get done no matter how overwhelming it seems. Your brain suddenly kicks into efficiency mode.

Squabbles about minor issues are tossed aside and bigger issues aren't a barrier anymore. Remember that one return you had to get out by April 15th? On April 10th, it seemed hopeless, but by April 11th, you threw caution to the wind, got the client on the phone, didn't take any excuses, got the documents you needed, and pumped out the return.

That's Parkinson's Law.

Now, compare that to what is done on a regular basis:

1. You get a client file. It sits for a bit.
2. A team member picks it up. There's missing information, so an email is shot off to the client.
3. Two weeks later, no word. Another email.
4. The CPA does a bit more work on the file as one document comes in, but they are still waiting on more.

You can see where this is going.

Suddenly, two months later, the work is about 75% done and when the client calls, disgruntled. You quickly sweep the problems aside and finish it.

This is reactive workflow. It's not good; it's inefficient and makes clients frustrated.

What you need to do is, with each project that comes in, set a deadline right away. Thirty days from now, the work will be complete. All documents are received upfront and you get it to the client on Day 20. That's great service.

1040 Process Sheet

Job or Service: _____   Date in: _____
Client Name: _____   Target Date Out: _____
Client Contact Info: _____   Actual Date Out: _____
Price to Client: _____   Price to Client: _____
Budgeted Hours: _____   Target Turnaround: _____
Partner: _____   Due Date: _____
Manager: _____   Extension Date: _____
Additional Team Members: _____
File Information: _____

Status:
Urgency:

Document File(s):

Task: _____   Owner: _____   Due: _____
Task: _____   Owner: _____   Due: _____
Task: _____   Owner: _____   Due: _____
Task: _____   Owner: _____   Due: _____
Task: _____   Owner: _____   Due: _____
Task: _____   Owner: _____   Due: _____
Task: _____   Owner: _____   Due: _____

Notes & Comments

Client Address or Billable Information:

Main Contact:
Secondary Contact:
Payment Method:
Payment Terms:

Budgeted Hours: Actual Hours: Actual Turn:
Internal Cost: Client Price: Profit Margin:

Jetpack Workflow

Figure 1: Process Sheet Example

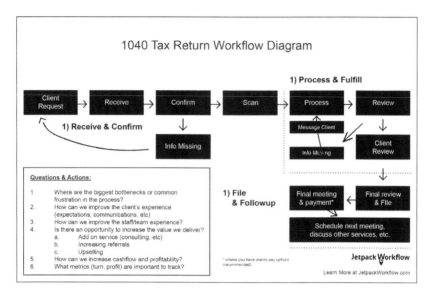

Figure 2: Workflow Diagram Example

Now, to get Parkinson's Law working at its maximum potential, you need to set the right processes in place to open up capacity and utilization.

Capacity and Utilization

When you open up capacity for your team to take on more work, you can bring in new clients while still nurturing your legacy clients. The former leads to more revenue without hiring more people. The latter leads to more referrals.

Dustin Hostetler, Director of Six Sigma Consulting and Boomer Consulting, breaks out teams to discuss processes.

> *"Just because a process is written down on paper doesn't mean it's reality."*

Here's how Dustin would get the system in motion: start with workflow visualization. To get started, he recommends getting a whiteboard or post-it notes together. Create a workflow map of your top three service categories.

Start at a 10,000-foot level and with the main steps and map them out on the whiteboard. This starts with, "Return goes from CPA to manager, to partner, to admin."

Those are the basics. Now, dig deeper.

Break each step into more detailed sub-steps. This is when you want each person involved in the step to sit down together, without the boss around, and outline their process. What you'll notice is they don't all have the same steps or processes. Now you know you have a problem. Let each member go over the issues they find. Nothing is fixed until every step and every member has the same process.

Damien Greathead, VP of Receipt Bank, sees these issues in firms every day. Often, practitioners are running around from office to office trying to get answers. But clients don't see the craziness, all they see is that their project isn't done on time.

He recommends, if you need to know where the bottlenecks are...

Ask the admin team. Administrative staff
ALWAYS know where the trouble spots are.

While you discuss all of this with your team, the questions you should be asking are:

1. How is the client experiencing our workflow? Where are they confused/angry/disappointed?

2. Where is my team stuck?

3. What is the most time consuming or frustrating part of this workflow?

4. Is there any part of the workflow where we can lower accounts receivable and get paid faster?

Map all these questions out through each step. The important piece to remember is, just because it is written down as part of the process does not mean it is actually happening that way! You will be able to figure this out based on the answers team members give for the above questions.

After talking over these points, ask (in this order):

1. What can we remove to save us time?

2. What processes do we need to update or clarify so the entire team has a uniform process?

3. Do we need to add any new steps? (This should always be last.)

Getting these questions answered is critical for increasing turnaround time and opening up capacity.

Going hand-in-hand with capacity is utilization. Utilization covers how much of the team's time is spent on client-facing, income-generating activities. As I discussed at the beginning of this chapter, you have certain duties depending on your position. Anything outside of those duties is inefficient and most likely not profitable for the firm.

If you use the billable hour as your metric, you can see right away the number of "unbilled" and "non-billable hours." Those should be as low as possible.

Do the quick math. Take all the non-billable hours from all your team members and multiply by their hourly rate and see how much revenue is being left behind.

Getting Started with Utilizing Your Time Efficiently

For one week, map, in detail, what you are doing with your time. Include every minute not spent working and every minute spent scrambling around looking for a document. Have your entire team do this.

Take a week to compare each member's schedule. Make sure your team feels comfortable putting down everything, rather than embellishing. It's important to explain, upfront, that there are no repercussions in any way, and that your goal is to help them make more money and work with better clients, not to assess their quality or usefulness. If you position it this way, they are much less likely to see it as a "Big Brother" project.

Dissect each member's time and find where the problem spots are:

- Is there too much down time?
- Is the team working too many hours?
- Are there similarities in problems they face?

Those are just a sample of the questions you could and should ask. Especially as an owner/partner in a firm, this step is critical. Your time is so incredibly valuable and you must find where you can cut out unproductive time. You will be surprised how much low-value time you are spending.

Later in the chapter, I'll give you some tools and tricks to start saving more time.

Onboarding Clients Correctly

Boosting efficiency is easiest to start with new clients. The absolute worst thing you can do is bring clients in through the same broken systems.

Stacy Kildal, founder of StacyK Academy, which helps bookkeepers grow their practice, found that once she instituted the right onboarding process, she was able to cut her client list down. Now, she has a waiting list. This was due to setting the right expectations and being efficient with putting the systems in place. Clients appreciate it and are willing to pay more.

Typically, managers and, at times, partners should do the initial onboarding process. Make sure you bring in the CPA who will handle the bulk of the workload so they can be up to speed as well.

To be effective at onboarding clients, you need to go in with a game plan and the confidence to have control of the discussion. Upfront, you'll want to lay out:

- Expectations for engagement
- What the client values
- What they can expect from you

We will discuss sales in a later chapter, but this runs parallel with how you go through a sales appointment. When you set the expectations for the call, prospects are more willing to walk to the beat of your drum because there is a plan in place.

In sales, the one who maintains control normally ends up getting what they want. Onboarding is the same. Yes, you already closed the client, but now you must further sell your process.

Right away, you should set the expectations for how they can become a good client. In the grand scheme of things, you shouldn't bring on clients that aren't going to go along with you; you'll lose profits and time.

You should set the expectations that:

- When the firm requests documents, the client will send those documents within one week, or whichever duration you are comfortable with.
- The firm is not a bean-counter, but a partner; one that helps grow their business.
- Team members are to be treated with respect at all times.
- If, at any time, one side doesn't feel they are receiving the right attention, schedule a call to address concerns.

These are just examples of the expectations you can set. You need to figure out who might be a great client for you and your team. We will touch more on this later, but it's important, if you have a new client coming in today, to make sure you are setting the right expectations.

Next, you need to listen to what your client values. Some clients value punctuality, while others value regular phone calls. Each client is as similar as they are different, so knowing them will help you serve them better.

These are the various touchpoints your CPAs will be making note of during the onboarding process: to make sure they over-deliver and get work early if the client values punctuality, to send quick emails each week if they prefer constant communication. As much as you see similarities between clients because they are the same industry, there will be small differences that your clients will appreciate you taking care of.

The last part of setting up the right onboarding process is letting the client know what they can expect. After hearing what a client values, you want to make sure you parrot back to them what they want. It shows you are listening and being attentive to their needs.

Most likely, your client picked your firm because you have a unique service or value. If you're local and you make sure your clients are your friends, tell the new client this. If you're known for the extra value in helpful information, let them know they can expect that as well.

These are the sprinkles on the ice cream. Remember, a new client is just as nervous as you are. They want to make sure they entrusted their financial future in the right hands. Any extra benefits help them feel more at ease in every way.

Stacy Kildal has her own method of onboarding that you can take as a great example. As an owner of a bookkeeping firm, she starts with a "Quick Review" of a client's books. She charges them right away for this so they actually value it, because, as you should know, we value what we pay for. By going through this upfront with a client, she's eliminated clients who weren't a good fit and who she knew would suck time out of her firm later.

For her next step, she prepares a quick report of what needs to be cleaned up. Since she's added this value, the client will most likely just hand over the work to her. She then makes sure she gets all the documentation to complete the work upfront. This saves time by eliminating going back and forth with the client.

The best way to approach onboarding clients is not to start with, "Let's get the clock moving so we can bill them." Rather, focus on ensuring they know what to expect and they understand the value you offer. It's a partnership, but it's also your business. Make sure the client is willing to work with you as well.

Should I Trim My Client Base?

If you onboard clients correctly, find where the bottlenecks are in the processes, and open up capacity for your team, you should be able to grow.

Here's a secret: when you get the systems working and you're providing value to your client, they will pay more. When they pay more, you will make more revenue per client. When you onboard a client correctly, then have the right processes to provide the most value to them, your firm is now *invaluable* to your client.

Putting in a new process isn't simple. It takes buy-ins, killing old habits, and recognition from clients. All of this can take time and frustration.

Here's what I recommend and what I've learned from talking to hundreds of firm owners: sometimes, you will need to cut a client loose for the good of the team and the process. Obviously, each client holds a certain "revenue spot" on the firm chart, but I'm talking about long-term growth and prospects. In a service business, it can be difficult to see where the profit gets lost. I'm here to tell you, a bad client costs much more in time and profits than you think. Cut a client loose if they don't conform with your new processes.

Chad Davis, a Partner at LiveCA, uses an internal metric called a "mushy point." Basically, each client is weighed not just on the revenue brought into the firm but also on how each team member enjoys working with them.

There will always be new clients out there, but building a new team because of high employee turnover is much harder. Ensuring your employees are satisfied with the clients they work for makes it easier to keep your staff and find the clients that suit your company. At LiveCA, they turn the idea into an equation, which gives the entire firm an idea of how valuable each client is.

I'm not saying you need to have "mushy points," but weighing all the things a client brings to the table isn't a bad idea. Remember, one bad client could chase a team member off.

Ingrid Edstrom, founder of Polymath, realized 30% of her client base was taking up most of her time. Most wanted a bunch of discounts and freebies, plus they were just not pleasant to work with.

One evening, she emailed the 30% telling them she was going in a different direction with her firm and referred them all to other firms. She made a tough decision to leave those clients and save her profits and team. Less than a year later, she doubled her business. All with clients she loves because she onboards them correctly.

She took the step back to make sure her home base was good, then took three steps forward. Now, her firm continues to grow. That's the difference between top firms and firms that putter along.

Tools & Tricks

By now, you should have assessed where there are hiccups in your process. Is technology a problem?

If you are still using outdated software, it's time to invest. A major downfall of more traditional firms is their use of paper. This isn't a green initiative, but a productivity one. Find a solution to keep everything digital and in a cloud server.

There are too many firms with file rooms filled with client documents, or a room holding their personal server. Those standards are over 10 years old and technology has changed quite a lot in the past decade. Now, there are multiple paperless options you can use to increase productivity and reduce physical space.

Tim Shortsleeve, Partner at TYS LLP and AICPA speaker, gave each of his employees a second monitor and saw a massive boost in productivity.

Another big push is toward cloud accounting and software. QuickBooks Online and Xero are great examples of where client books could be. When you can get every new client online, everything runs smoother because there's just one process to follow.

A friend of mine came from a firm where every client was different. They wanted to "cater to the client's wants." Yes, you should do this, but not at the expense of profit and increased frustration. At his firm, one client was on QB Online, another on QB 2015, yet another QB 2013, and even one on Peachtree accounting.

You can't run a firm like this. If it's a cost issue for your client, it might be worth it for you to pay for them to upgrade, ensuring all your clients are on the same system. My friend would waste countless hours tracking down other team members asking "Why can't I do this in QB 2010 but I can in QB 2014, what do I do?"

You can't grow a firm like that, so make it a demand: *all new clients will be on cloud accounting.*

Since we're on the topic of technology, here are some recommended apps that save you non-billable and unproductive time. I use these myself and can't tell you how much time they've saved me.

- **Calendly:** This app integrates your calendar and lets you send a personalized link to anyone to schedule a time with you. It saves the regular "What time works for you?" emails.
- **Team Hively:** It's an automated feedback tool sent to your clients. The information you gather is priceless and helps you strengthen your processes. Plus, it's all automated.

- **Flux:** This is more of an "underground" hack. Flux dims the light on your computer and removes the blue light. This keeps your eyes from getting tired, especially when working late.
- **Followup.cc:** This one is absolutely essential for retrieving client documents. It allows you to simply set a template and let it automatically send emails to clients to remind them to send documents. It saves you hours per month following up on missing information.
- **Temporary site blockers:** There are many to choose from. I've used rescuetime.com to keep employees focused. It doesn't need to be something employees are scared of, but more of an internal way to measure how much time is wasted by distractions. Let team members use it privately so they can adjust their habits on their own.

Conclusion

You might have been tempted to skip over this chapter and get to the more "juicy" pieces, like getting new clients and referrals, but you'll be glad you didn't get too far ahead of yourself. Now, you know that you could get as many clients as you want, but if you don't build out the right systems, you'll experience these issues:

- Clients will be unhappy and some will leave.
- You will be working day and night.
- Your team won't stay together, so you'll waste precious time hiring and training.

These are just facts. In football, games are won in the trenches. The quarterback, running backs, and wide receivers get the glory, but if you don't take care of the offensive line, it won't matter.

You need the "less sexy" things taken care of first before you go out and find new clients. You'll feel more comfortable bringing in bigger clients, plus you won't be waking up in the middle of the night thinking "Did I miss something?"

Have each level of your firm follow these pieces of advice: partners, *stop* spending time on admin tasks; managers, *stop* getting lost in the weeds and keep the system alive; practitioners, trust the process; and administrative staff, take as much as you can off the plates of the partners.

This is how firms grow.

P.S. For Partners

Partners are the reason new systems don't get implemented. They might have gotten used to 20 years of doing it their way and refuse to change. Here is my plea to you: I understand you're very good at what you do. You make a living this way because you enjoy it and it pays well. A new system will have you spend more time out with your family and get you more dividends at year-end.

Doing it your own way only makes it harder for everyone else and for the younger team members who look up to you for guidance.

Changing habits is tough. It's not because you can't do your job, it's just that times and technology change. There are better ways. You're supposed to be a leader in the firm and are responsible for its growth. Put pride aside and work together.

Damien Greathead has a hard and fast rule: if a partner is resistant to change that grows the firm, they have to go...

Action Steps

1. Define the roles of everyone in the firm. What will each person be doing?

2. Ask yourself, how can we implement a standard turnaround time for projects to take advantage of Parkinson's Law?

3. Sit down with your team and go through the processes. Where are the trouble spots?

4. Map each person's time. Where are there openings and where are the bottlenecks?

5. Re-examine the onboarding process for a new client. Are we bringing in the right clients and finding a way to cut out the bad?

6. Look at your own client base. Are there clients who aren't contributing to our firm or hurting us?

Interviews to Go Deeper

1. Build a Better Workflow - with Jeff Borcshowa (https://jetpackworkflow.com/how-to-build-a-better-workflow-accounting-practice/)

2. Landing the Best Clients - with Stacy Kildal (https://jetpackworkflow.com/3-steps-to-landing-the-best-bookkeeping-clients/)

3. Ditch Timesheets and Grow Quickly - with Tim Shortsleeve (https://jetpackworkflow.com/grow-a-successful-accounting-practice/)

4. Mastering Workflow for Firms - with Damien Greathead (https://jetpackworkflow.com/mastering-workflow-for-accountants-cpa-damien-greathead-interview/)

5. Boost your Firm Profitability - with Rob Nixon (https://jetpackworkflow.com/accounting-firm-profitability-rob-nixon/)

6. Apply Lean Six Sigma to Workflow - with Dustin Hostetler (https://jetpackworkflow.com/applying-lean-six-sigma-to-your-workflow-the-dustin-hostetler/)

7. Double Revenues by Cutting 30% of Clients - with Ingrid Edstrom (https://jetpackworkflow.com/double-bookkeeping-revenue/)

8. Onboard New Clients - with Chad Davis (https://jetpackworkflow.com/how-to-onboard-new-clients-manage-a-remote-team-the-chad-davis-interview/)

Recommendations

I've spent years building software to solve these exact issues. My company, Jetpack Workflow (https://app.jetpackworkflow.com/), is used around the world to prevent work from falling through the cracks and to ensure you keep your clients happy.

If this chapter struck a chord with you, it probably means you have holes in your workflow processes. I invite you to try a 14-day free trial of Jetpack (https://app.jetpackworkflow.com/users/sign_up). No obligation required.

Too many firms live on outdated software and it ruins efficiency and limits capacity. You're reading this book to grow your firm, and your workflow processes act as your foundation. It's the most important change you can make.

You can also email me: david@jetpackworkflow.com

Chapter 2

Solving the Pricing Problem

Janice's firm was in a rut. They were gaining new clients, but had a hard time maintaining profitability. It struck him as odd, as this 30-year-old accounting firm hadn't changed much in their practice. They continued to have a similar size staff and good client growth, so what was causing the drop in profits?

At their monthly C-level meeting, Janice asked his technology lead why, given all the improvements in their technology infrastructure, profitability was actually going down.

Upon digging into the numbers, and—most critically—talking with staff, he realized one thing:

> *Staff was incentivized to get maximum billable hours without going over budget, so they commonly skipped work or duplicated the tools that were automating their practice.*

Your profits ride on whether your team members are willing to sit at their desk just a bit longer. In today's climate as a CPA, it doesn't need to be this way. You simply can't afford it.

If Janice's story resonates with you, you're not alone. The idea of "billing for time" has been around for a while. In fact, the only common scenario we hear is that firms simply do not adopt useful and efficient applications because of they decrease billable time. What inevitably happens is that a competitor will charge a lower price for equal—or often greater—service, and your firm will no longer be competitive in the modern market.

With the push of automation and ongoing efficiency, a firm focused solely on the billable hour is one that seemingly continues to struggle in today's marketplace.

Now, **I'm not saying to move entirely to a value-based, zero-timesheet practice tomorrow; absolutely not. Always think strategically about your pricing model before jumping ship.** Instead, I'll walk you through the alternatives you can choose for your firm, plus the benefits you will see. You will also learn how to move your current and new clients into this pricing model without running into issues.

Price. It's such an emotional and psychological topic for many business owners. Price has many elements, but before we dive into tactics, let's dive into one thing first: mindset

Mindset

If you do not value the service you provide to your clients and understand the ROI of the services you offer, it's extremely hard to make a price increases or transitions.

Or if you do not believe little ole' me can ever demand a higher price point, simply because you believe you're not supposed to, then these pricing strategies will not make an impact.

In fact, while things like market positioning, price positioning, proper sales consulting, and marketing all go into demanding a higher fee, many firm owners never start the process. Or nearly as bad, they take one small action, fail, and then never return.

So before we dive into price, let's complete the following exercise:

1. If you and all other accounting firms were to go under today, and individuals and small business owners had to do their accounting themselves, what would happen? What would happen to their time? Their cash flow? Their profitability? Their sanity?

2. For those firms who do charge more, what allows them to ask for more? Note: you cannot point to location, years in business, size of staff, office type, etc. The question is: how are they perceived by a market that *expects either a higher price or different pricing model?*

The reason we start with mindset is because without the belief in your product or service, a pricing strategy will not work. Whether it's an hourly increase or a move to fixed or value-based pricing, you need to become grounded in the value—both perceived and actual—that you bring to a client.

If no one else has, I give you permission to think outrageously high of your service and ability to help clients. I give you permission to ask for higher fees and experiment with new billing models.

In this chapter, we're going to highlight practitioners who made the exact same journey and what they did to make the transition. We're going to look to thought leaders who have helped hundreds of firm owners make the transition. Big and small, new and old, "hip" and conservative.

Remember, price is about a transfer of value, *both* perceived and actual.

> *What's the difference between perceived and actual?*
>
> Perceived: "This accounting firm has helped so many successful companies, we're bound to be successful as well."
>
> Actual: "Their quick turnaround time and simple cash flow reports make it easy to see if we're on the right track every month."

You play in the world of both, and therefore pricing does as well. Take these next chapters as permission to review and update your pricing model. At the end of the chapter, you'll find links to the interviews we've referenced throughout this section.

Why Move Away from the Billable Hour?

The emergence of the Internet has disrupted every industry. You knew that. But in professional services, it turned your service offering on its head because your expertise is more valuable than ever before.

When you don't know something, you whip out your smartphone and google the answer. Even your older clients take full advantage of having intelligence in their hand 24/7. When they wish to tap into your intelligence, they want to feel they aren't taking a massive risk.

The billable hour works such that: *"I charge you for my time. Period."* Suddenly, you evolve into a time-punching machine.

"Lawyer Bob is calling... David, you are now on the clock..."

Don't you believe, deep down, you are worth more than your hours?

Of course.

You spent years, maybe decades, developing your craft. You spent late nights studying for certifications. You've done your time of messing up client work and now know better.

Those are all valuable! You become a better partner, CPA, and accounting expert with all of this experience downloaded and backed up in your head. You deserve payment for it.

As you get better, the common idea is to simply peg your time as more valuable. You go from $200 per hour to $215 per hour. Think about it. Over 100 hours, you make an extra $1,500.

Woopie!

Malcolm Gladwell's *Outliers*, proposes the famous 10,000-hour rule. In other words, it takes 10,000 before you become an expert. When you become an expert, you know more than 99% of people in the world.

That's worth something. But, it's not worth it in the currency of time.

When you go to the doctor, you are seeking counsel. You get the bill in the mail. What do you see? Nowhere does it say: "Dr. Bill Able saw you for one hour; your charge is $X." No. You are charged for what they did. The more valuable the service, the more they charged.

A routine check-up bills out at the lowest tier. It's the least valuable. Cancer treatment and life-saving surgery—no matter how short it was—can cost tens of thousands of dollars.

As you harvest the more specialized knowledge of a doctor, the fee skyrockets. Unfortunately for them, insurance companies will negotiate some of their fee away. Fortunately for you, you don't have to deal with insurance at your firm.

The point is, the shift away from the billable hour has happened because your expertise is more valuable than ever. Your clients are paying for outcomes; they aren't paying for how long you spend on a project.

Let me be more blunt: *they don't care how long it takes you.*

If it took five minutes, great. If it took your whole weekend and you missed your child's school play, sorry.

I do the same thing now for all the work I do and hire other people for. I negotiate the price upfront. When a plumber comes to my house, I ask, *"What's this going to cost?"* The buyer now has power because of the Internet. I know, roughly, how much a leaky faucet is going to cost.

The plumber is now strapped because it may take him three hours or it could take him three minutes. This is the issue both you and your clients face with the billable hour: you're incentivized to take as long as you can.

In my plumbing example, the plumber, to match online competitors, lowballs himself to get the job. He's afraid if he does a bad job, I'll post it on Yelp. So he takes his time, does the job, and gets paid the bottom of the barrel for his work.

This is where CPA firms struggle in terms of getting the most revenue per client. If your client sees you as a commodity to be bargained with, you will lose. It's up to you to demonstrate the value you bring to the table.

Your value is your expertise! If that plumber said, *"As a free bonus, let me do an audit of your house, I can see where you might be able to add some value,"* he would be positioning himself as more valuable and would be able to charge more. Do you see the difference?

Heck, if he knew me more, he would know to dig deeper and say, *"I know you're selling your house soon, there are a few things you can do to add some profit to the bottom line."* This just keeps getting better! Value, value, value. No longer is this plumber a commodity; he is a trusted expert.

This is what your clients are quietly screaming for. This is why the billable hour continues to go the way of the dinosaur. The landscape has changed forever. Your clients signed with you, not for your time, but for a partnership. They receive full access to your database of knowledge, you get paid, and your firm grows. Your clients open their wallets for outcomes, not time.

This is a massive mindset shift. It requires a bit of boldness, as well. Becoming a firm of the future starts with charging for outcomes. It's how you will differentiate yourself from your competitors.

The Difference between Time, Fixed and Value Pricing

According to Ron Baker, world-renowned expert on value pricing for CPA firms, *"Billable hours breed uncertainty."*

Your clients are often scared to give you new projects because they are afraid of the bill. Ironically, you have the same fear going to the ER, but unfortunately for you, a client's taxes aren't directly life or death.

As a vendor, you should be taking on the risk for a project, but with the billable hour, the risk rests on your client's shoulders. Every phone call, whether you have an answer for them or not, they still get billed. Every project that takes 20 hours longer than originally budgeted, they still get billed.

Soon, your client is afraid to call you for fear of paying for wasted time. They then pull up a search engine and try to locate the answer themselves. That doesn't lead to problems, does it…?

The most successful companies in the world take the risk on their shoulders every day. Apple builds a new iPhone each year. If it's not what people want, nobody buys it and they lose billions in development and manufacturing. Google gives its search engine away for free. If they don't give great results and improve it every day, no one will click on their ads and all other projects, like Google maps, Android, and Chrome will suffer and cease to exist. Zappos, a billion-dollar shoe company, will ship shoes to you for free. If you don't like them, you ship them back for free. Zappos loses money. Your local grocery store wholesales select goods and puts them on the shelves for you to browse for free. If no one buys a certain brand of milk, your grocery store loses money.

That's how businesses become trusted, household names: they take the risk.

Imagine if you are in the market for a house and at every house you walk through, your realtor charges you. Buying a house is a massive decision and you don't want to be rushed, but you are cramped for time because your realtor has you on the clock.

The real estate industry would implode as more homebuyers would take on the risk of buying a home on their own, without an expert. This is why realtors are paid on commission. We pay them thousands in commission for their expertise and the result, not for their time.

Why wouldn't you do the same?

"Hourly billing doesn't fit the knowledge economy."
—Ron Baker

Let's look at the equation for hourly billing:

- Hourly billing = people (capacity) * efficiency (realization, utilization, billable) * hourly rate.

To use it as an example. Let's look at New Hire Steve.

New Hire Steve starts his Monday with about 6 hours of billable time to use. The rest will go to non-billable activities. Because he is new, it took him an hour longer than normal to complete a regular tax return for one of your clients, Dr. Hunter Bargain. New Hire Steve's hourly rate as a new CPA is $100.

Put it in our equation:

- 6 hours * 90% (tax return normally bills 5.5 hours and Steve took 6) * $100 = $540 for the day ($60 is written off.)

At the end of the year, New Hire Steve will hopefully get his efficiency rate back over 100%. If so, they will raise his hourly rate. If not, it would not make profitable sense to raise it, but they will need to give him a raise due to precedence. So whether he increases his efficiency or not, your expenses increase. If his efficiency remains the same, his profitability goes down even further. The billable hour doesn't maximum the value of New Hire Steve getting smarter and better while increasing your firm profits. It's a broken system.

Let's look at how fixed pricing compares.

Fixed pricing is essentially charging, as it states, a fixed amount per month for your services. This pricing is great if you are doing similar tasks each month for a client.

You would define the terms and scope of the project within certain parameters and agree to re-visit at pre-determined intervals. This is where you start to take the risk off your client's shoulders. You can introduce a service that gives your client complete access to your services at any time, plus add in value points as you go.

Getting to a fixed price runs parallel with a Cost-Plus model. In this model, you take what you estimate the cost might be in terms of time and resources. Then, you tack on the profit margin you wish to hit.

Let's go back to New Hire Steve. He has the same hourly rate of $100 per hour and the same tax return that will take 6 hours.

The final discussions with the client before embarking on the project will include, *"Your tax return, all-in for you, will cost $895. This will include all our phone calls, any questions you may have during the process as well as tips I can give you along the way."*

Suddenly, the tax return you billed $540 for is worth $895. For arguments sake, let's say you have an extra hour of time your client now enjoys of consulting over the phone, plus you spent 15 minutes writing an email with some tips for the following year.

That's an extra $125 you would've charged for hourly billing. On an hourly bill, that's $665 as compared to the fixed price of $895. That's almost a 30% increase in revenue.

Then, as New Hire Steve becomes more efficient, the return will only take 5 hours and, because the client will have the tips from the prior year, he will require less time on the phone. Yet, you can still charge $895. Or, you can show the value you created and bump up the price to $1000 and the client would still pay because of the service and value you create.

Think of when you buy tickets for a flight across the country. An airline operates much like fixed pricing. They take the cost and add in their profit to get the price of your ticket. As demand and gasoline prices fluctuate, the profit margin wavers. The airline isn't charging per hour. It would be too easy to find out if you are getting taken for a ride! No, instead, the prices of tickets are still a mystery.

We know they aren't calculated at value pricing, because that is more customized to the customer. If someone is trying to buy a ticket to race to their mother's side as she passes away within the day, value pricing would mean the passenger would pay *much* more for a ticket than perhaps someone flying to see their in-laws for the holidays, but the price remains the same, despite the circumstances. That is fixed pricing.

Going back to the CPA firm world, you can see the differences between the billable hour and fixed pricing. There's no doubt you have questions bubbling up about efficiency and keeping employees on point. Those are everyone's first questions, but let's touch more on value pricing first, before we will get to your other concerns.

Value pricing strips away all elements of time and goes to the core of the issue, *"How much is this solution worth to you?"* Value pricing is ultra-powerful when it comes to one-time projects, as you can gain maximum profit, but ongoing projects can still see a benefit.

The difference, first of all, between fixed pricing and value pricing is what you base the pricing on and the perception you create. Fixed pricing is more about pricing each service, while value pricing digs into the value of your services to your clients. Think of it as, "This service costs $X," vs, "How much is this service worth to you?"

Both are much more profitable than the billable hour and can be used at different points and with different clients. The fixed pricing model would be the easiest first step to get out of billing for time. It's easier to understand and much more straightforward.

Value pricing, though, is personal. It digs deep into each individual client to get at what they truly care about and assigning value to it. The power of value pricing is you can charge much more while working less. Hourly billing is solely focused on how much time you sit at your desk or cubicle. Value pricing is all about the *result* for the client.

When the pain point for a client is big enough, they are willing to pay as much as needed to get rid of the issue. Think about when you had your first child (or, when someone you know had a child.) Imagine if complications come up during the final week of the pregnancy. They bring you in with a specialist for delivering babies in distress. The parents of the child have a massive need—they want their first child to be born as healthy as possible with the least amount of trouble for both the mother and child.

Suddenly, the specialist's value is worth much more. Instead of charging $X per hour, or simply a flat fee, the specialist can charge with value pricing because these parents are willing to put up any amount of money to make the birth go as near perfect as possible.

How much more could you charge?

Immediately, you might think of extortion. In the firm world, it's not as dramatic as childbirth, but there are problems clients face that they wish would just go away.

Jackson runs an audit practice, and they've seen massive growth since switching to value pricing. How?

Well, like many, he used to charge around $150–$300 per hour. Over time, he realized his clients would do anything to not get audited by the IRS.

Jackson saw an opportunity to not just prepare audits, but to provide consultations to his clients about prepping and accounting for everything with the goal of removing as many red flags as possible and avoid getting audited in the first place. Every month, he does a "Red Flag check" for his clients.

Audits can cost tens of thousands of dollars. Now, he charges what he used to charge, about $3,500 per audit, but, he bundles it with another $5,000 annually to do his "Red Flag check" each month. This check takes him about an hour to do, and it gets easier as he does it.

Now, he hands it off to a junior staff member to do it and he pockets almost $4,000 in extra profits due to the value he provided. Then, his audit goes even faster the next year, saving him even more time and increasing his profits further! He was able to charge the $5,000 because if his client did get audited, they typically ended up paying much more in taxes than they thought. Not to mention, the miscellaneous costs that get thrown in.

His clients are willing to pay that extra amount as Jackson attaches a guarantee: *"If you get audited and end up paying any more in taxes, we will foot the entire tax bill and the costs."*

Look at that value! The risk is completely off the client and is put on Jackson's firm to do the best possible job. This is the power of value pricing. You aren't being paid for your time, but for your expertise. You are in this industry because you love the details and numbers and analysis that is accounting. Get paid for it.

Let's look at the equation for value pricing:

- Value pricing = intellectual capital * effectiveness * price

Intellectual capital has three components:

- **Human capital:** The actual knowledge and expertise you've garnered that can't be replaced if you leave.
- **Social capital:** Your vendors, associations, clients, employees etc.
- **Structural capital:** The physical pieces of the business, the processes, the strategies, and the workflow.

With value pricing, you are charging for everything you bring to the table, not just time. Time is going to pass anyway. The knowledge you and your team hold is something difficult to duplicate.

Benefits of Fixed Pricing

Fixed pricing allows you to turn off the clock and run your practice with predictable revenue. If you are charging a client $1,000 a month to help them with their books, it's predictable. You know you will take home $12,000 in bookkeeping fees.

This allows for easier budgeting.

Your clients breathe easier knowing all help and services can fit neatly into a fixed payment. They can budget easier and happily keep you updated on their business because they aren't on the clock. You might wonder why your clients don't tell you about big events in their business and you don't hear about it until the tax deadline. It's probably because they didn't want to be charged for it.

Fixed pricing takes time out of the equation, meaning your managers are spending less time each week paging through timesheets and, instead, are working on keeping cracks out of the process and workflow, which is their main goal.

Your teams will improve each month with the processes, so work will take less time, but you are still getting paid the full amount. Then, you open up capacity and allow new clients to fill in the gaps, and the process repeats.

Many of these benefits mirror what you will see with value pricing.

Benefits of Value Pricing

It's believed over 90% of workers are not paid what they are worth. We undercut ourselves. Value pricing positions what you do compared to the needs of your client. Professional services, like a CPA firm, have very few assets. There are a bunch of computers, but no power plants or manufacturing equipment. The biggest asset you have is your human capital; your knowledge.

Value pricing captures payment for that knowledge, disregarding the time spent. The most powerful "little things" in business are ideas. Your financial know-how has ideas that could change your client's company. Those are valuable. Time and effort are *not* valuable to the client.

Think about a heart surgeon. How valuable is one when you have a cold? Not very. That's not where the surgeon's expertise is. He could spend an hour with you trying to prescribe the right medication, but that's not what you pay him for.

What about if your heart isn't pumping correctly and you require surgery? Suddenly, this heart surgeon is the most valuable person in the world to call. The surgeon can charge much more, due to his expertise, than 99% of the people in the world who don't have that same experience.

Heart surgeons get paid more than a general practitioner and work less. Their skill is so valuable that one surgery would be worth more than the average practitioner's monthly salary.

See the value? You must think of yourself the same way. You have important knowledge and the ability to execute on that knowledge to get results. You can charge much more for your services than you do. It's all just about positioning yourself in your client's mind.

In addition, billable hour billing requires you to actually do the work before accepting payment. Then, you end up spending many hours throughout the year tracking down client payments. Value pricing has you paid upfront to get money out of the way. Your Accounts Receivable department will take a big hit, but that's always a good thing!

Clients will gladly pay upfront because you will be providing more value than they expect. You will see, in later steps, how you can add extra value they might not have known they needed as part of the package. Those extra services will be high-margin and simple for you to perform, but high-value to your clients.

Ready to start taking the next big step?

Converting Clients to Fixed Pricing, then Value Pricing

I recommend first moving your new clients to fixed pricing, just to get your feet wet. The conversations you have with clients will be completely different and it takes practice.

You *will not* knock it out of the park the first time.

You need to know how to the approach the conversation in the right way to get clients to understand where you are going. You've read about the benefits of going this route and you've picked up this book because you are trying to grow your firm.

Theory is fun to read about, but executing successfully is where results come from. Wherever on the growth line you are, you can tap into this and implement it. Remember, fixed and value pricing models open up capacity for your team, while also exploding the revenue per client. No longer are you tracking your time and billing for each hour you work. Instead, you are cashing in on your expertise and strategies, and turning those into outcomes for your clients.

Before we dive in, it's imperative to know that this is powerful. Firms have changed virtually overnight using value pricing. But here is a gentle reminder: you must have the right workflow and processes in place for this to work. Your inside must be running smoothly before messing with your outward activities.

If you haven't gone through Step 1, *do not* start implementing these strategies just yet. Your foundation must be set before building.

Actual Steps to Make the Switch

Steve Major, podcast host at Pricing Power and "timesheet killer," recommends giving 3–6 months before having your firm fully on fixed or value pricing. Meaning, slowly introduce it to new clients and your team, don't just go cold turkey.

This is its own process that needs nurturing and gradual acceptance from the team. Keep the timesheets in, but remove billable hours processes, bit by bit.

To start, list all your current services and offerings. Which services are not as profitable as you would like? Perhaps there are services you offer that many clients don't know about. This will be important when you present your new pricing scheme to them.

Next, you will go through each service and ask, *"Why do clients use this service?"* Is it for compliance? Is it to grow their company? List the benefits for each. Start seeing where you can bundle services.

When you look at an internet plan for your home, you can also bundle TV and phone and get the price for those individual services at a lower cost. The internet service provider makes a healthy margin on all three, no matter what and you simply pay one fee per month for all of it.

Those are the connections you are trying to make right now. As you know, if a client is getting bookkeeping done, you can bundle that with the tax return as you probably already do.

Now, get creative. Where else can you bundle in services? Is there a cash flow management service you could also bundle in? What about CEO management consulting?

Remember, clients don't know everything you do. You might think they do, but they don't. You might think you know everything a dentist does, but they do much more than just clean teeth and fill cavities.

It's not your client's job to figure out if you have a service. It's *your* job to introduce it.

In Front of a New Client

Armed with your list of primary and auxiliary services, only then can you take this next step to get in front of a client. Again, start with a new client who just signed. They have no preconceived notions about your firm, so it's the perfect time to practice before you discuss this new pricing model with your legacy clients.

Now, the more client industry knowledge you have, the more value you can bring to the table and the more you can charge.

In the opening, you want to get the client to agree upfront to, *"Mr. Client, we will only undertake this engagement if you agree to our mutual satisfaction that the value we are creating for you is worth more than what you pay us."*

Here, you are priming the client to agree to the steps you will lay out. As you will learn later, sales is all about leading the conversation. In this value conversation, you need to sell your pricing model.

Now, you need to start digging for what your client values. What drives them personally and professionally?

Kirk Bowman, notable "visionary of value," recommends asking naive questions. All you want at this point is to get the client chatting and you listening. Your goal is not to spring your service offerings. That's for much later.

Before you get to that step, you need to know what the client values and their "why." Why do they do what they do? Why did they build a business? Why do they keep going?

You won't get direct answers to these, you need to listen for hints. *"I'm excited to retire in the next ten years...My daughter will be off to college soon then law school...I'm looking at expanding to a second location..."*

All these are little hints at what they value and what they need. It takes time to learn how to listen, but you will get there. Some examples of questions you can ask a new client:

- Why did you switch to us?
- Why now?
- How are you currently solving the issue you mentioned?

- What frustrations do you have?
- What does a successful relationship with us look like for you?

Kirk Bowman also recommends pushing back a bit, as well, in order to discover their needs:

- Why are you doing this now and not six months from now?
- What's the cost if you do *nothing*?

Jason Blumer, firm owner and coach, mixes it up with more whimsical questions. Questions that get clients to have to think creatively. His favorite:

Imagine I am a Genie and you get three wishes. What do you want me to create, destroy, and blow up? Also, what are the dreams you have?

It's a fun question that can really disarm a new client. Disarming them leads to more honest and open answers. These questions are there to explore areas many firms never explore.

Throughout this part of the conversation, you should have your client speaking about 90% of the time. If a client feels uncomfortable answering any of these questions, try different whimsical questions to have them thinking differently. If they get upset, it's usually a red flag that they might not be a great fit for your firm.

You don't want to be the firm that accepts everyone. As we discussed in Chapter 1, one bad client can cause disruptions on your team, mess up your workflow, and steal capacity from more profitable clients. Unfortunately, onboarding for most firms simply involves order-taking.

"What do you need? Tax Returns? Ok, that will be $1,000, thanks for being a client."

This leads to bad client experiences, bad clients, and bad team management.

It's your firm. You choose who comes into your house and sits at your table. You wouldn't invite everyone. You would only want those who would be great guests. Treat your firm like your house. Be firm with new clients who don't want to play by the rules. If they don't, simply end the conversation, thank them for their time and tell them it's not a good fit. There are millions of companies out there, so don't be handcuffed by one.

Some business owners are used to being in control and like to maintain that control. You aren't interested in that. You know much more about finances, tax, and compliance than they do, no matter how much time they've spent in QuickBooks. If they don't value that, you will never get a good price from them and you won't be able to provide much value to them, anyway.

Pricing

You are probably wondering, *"Ok, when do we get to the pricing throwdown?"*

This is a delicate process you need to walk through. You will get better at it as you go, but you don't want it to be an order-taking process as you might be used to. This isn't fast-food dining. This is helping a business owner achieve his dreams.

You don't want to jump out into pricing too quickly. Kirk Bowman has seen *"The earlier you talk about price, the lower it will go."* This entire conversation is framing the client to think about getting the results they want and be open to investing in themselves rather than just *cost, cost, cost.*

Let the client nickel and dime his electrician or paper supplier. You aren't a bean-counter. You're a valuable partner, consultant, coach, advisor, friend, and expert. Which sounds better?

Mentioning price too early doesn't allow you to collect all the data you need to present a viable solution to the client.

It is only after you've defined their needs and dug deeper to see what they value most, their biggest concerns, and their pains, that you even touch price. Don't present the price until you've stepped back and evaluated what's best for them.

This dives into deep psychology. Your client has laid out all their pains and you've assured them you can solve their issues. At that point, the client wants to get going.

You then do something against the norm: you step back. You don't lay your cards out on the table. You leave the client nibbling at the bit to get going. When you feel that excitement from the client, you have put the puzzle together.

What are you doing stepping away? It lets you discuss the best options for the client. Notice I said "options."

As humans, we love being in control. When you give your client "options," you hand them the reins. For you, it goes much deeper. When someone is given an option, if they feel it is a good deal—they feel like they are getting more than what is being charged—so, they are compelled and seduced to buy it.

This is why you lay out all your services and try to find where some complement each other. Your new client might say, *"I just need bookkeeping."* Yet, after going through your value conversation, you believe cash flow management sessions might help them as well, so you add it as part of the option.

Ron Baker, the master of value pricing in CPA firms, believes three options are the best bet. Think about when you go to Starbucks, you get to choose the size of coffee you would like.

Which size do most people choose? You're right, the medium. It's also priced in a way that you *feel* you are getting a deal on it.

Ron calls your options Green, Gold & Platinum:

- **Green:** Very basic service they would need to get the job done.
- **Gold:** What you are nudging them to pick. Includes basic service + high-value and high-profit products or services you can include.
- **Platinum:** The "fist pump" selection including everything in Gold with some extras on top the client might not need but it may entice them to think, *"I may need that at some point."*

Platinum should be really stretching yourself, as Kirk believes. If you aren't stretching yourself, you aren't going to grow your firm. I promise you, no client is going to get upset you offered services you felt they might need. The worst they can say is, *"No thanks, I'll just do the Green package."*

This is how you grow your firm: exposing your services to your clients because they don't know everything you do.

> ***Extra tip:*** *Your goal is to get the client to pick the Gold package. In the example above, the client came in looking for a CPA to do his/*

her tax return, but left feeling they were getting a bargain with the tax return done and a better handle on cash flow.

To price, set the Green and Gold prices in the same ballpark. You want the client to feel they are getting a "steal" for the Gold price. Then, with the Platinum, you shoot the price up much higher. The idea behind this is the client will see the large Platinum price, look at the Gold price and it will look much smaller.

Let's use an example:

Your client is looking for a simple tax return and bookkeeping every month.

Here's how you could structure it:

	GREEN	GOLD	PLATINUM
Bookkeeping monthly	$2,000	$2,000	$2,000
Tax return (Business)	$1,000	$1,000	$1,000
Tax planning (Business)	N/A	FREE	$500
Cash flow management (6 one-hour sessions)	N/A	$3,500	$2,500
CFO consulting (6 two-hour sessions)	N/A	N/A	$5,000
Audit Protection (1x per month)	N/A	N/A	$1,000
24/7 access	$500 (1 hour per month)	FREE	FREE
TOTAL	**$3,500**	**$6,500**	**$12,500**

Notice where a client is going to get pulled to. For just $3,000 more, they get unlimited access to you, free tax planning, and help with cash flow.

What's the cost to you? The more you do with the client, the less you will end up talking with them per month, so the 24/7 access doesn't take much more time, but there's the allure and safety blanket of it.

Essentially, you give up six one-hour sessions over the entire year, plus the quick work of tax planning, which is much easier since you do their bookkeeping. So, you make an extra $3,000 with little extra work. Do that for 200 clients and that's $600,000 in additional revenues

Notice the Platinum price is much higher than the first two prices. Suddenly, $6,500 looks much smaller next to $12,500.

These are simple numbers, just as an example. Put in your own numbers and see the value you could create virtually overnight for your firm.

This is an exciting turning point for your firm, but I know you still have questions.

FAQ

With no timesheets, how do I know who is doing a good job and being productive?

This is the most common question. Steve Major believes if you look at turnaround time, you can see who is productive and who isn't. If you're being the best leader you can be for your team, you will *know* who is not pulling their own weight. Your managers will see where the cracks in the team are forming. It doesn't take much to see when one employee gets work in faster than others.

In Chapter 1, you mapped your time for the week to see where the inefficiencies are. Remember, you can't evaluate your pricing without first managing your workflow.

How do I have this conversation with current clients?

You'll want to start with your most trusted clients first. Tell them you are looking at your current service offerings and there might be some extra ways you can add value for them.

Also, describe how you are moving pricing models to be more efficient and get work out to them much faster. Show vulnerability that you are growing but also how it will benefit them as your client.

Next, simply go through similar value-digging questions. You'll learn more about your clients this way, plus you can ask for referrals at the end.

If you're still uncomfortable, call up your most trusted client and simply ask, *"Hi Mr. Client, we are making some changes in our pricing and service offerings. I am trying out a new way to present to clients. Can I have 20 minutes of your time to try it out on you and get your feedback?"*

This trial conversation could lead to more sales when your client says, *"I didn't know you did that!"*

What if a current client doesn't like this new way?

You ask yourself, *"How much value does this client bring to the firm?"* You can't have a client hold back your firm's growth. Your goal is growth or you wouldn't be reading this book.

We've found if you give the clients the option to walk and they like you, they will work out how they can stay. Clients don't want to look for another CPA!

How do I get the firm to buy into this?

First, just have them read this chapter. The firms who will grow are already doing this and you are behind. As younger CPAs come up the chain, they want more flexibility in their schedule. They don't want to be chained to their desk because they need 2500 billable hours for the year.

You will need to have a sit-down conversation with your partners who resist change. See the note at the end of Chapter 1. You will need to explain how staying put is hindering the firm. Those who will oppose will be the "old-timers." Those who are used to what they've done for 30 years. I'm not saying it won't be a tough conversation, but it's necessary or nothing in this book will be useful.

If you're happy with your firm, great. This book is for those who want to build a growing, successful, enjoyable firm without giving up everything else in life.

Conclusion

You've gotten the hard sell on why you need to ditch the billable hour for good. You will free up capacity and have less "debt-collecting," increased profits, more services being used, and better clients.

It all starts with your mindset. You are worth more and you don't need to lower your price because a prospect says so. You aren't going to nail fixed and value pricing on day one. You may set a price too low at first. You may ask for a price too high and scare a prospect away. It's only when you find that happy medium, matching what you charge to the budget of an ideal prospect, that will you be a happier, more profitable firm.

Start small with a few new clients. Move them to fixed pricing and then make the shift to value pricing. The results will astound you.

Action Steps

1. Ask yourself, do I firmly believe I'm worth more than other firms? You must have a "Yes" to this answer.

2. Recognize the differences and benefits between fixed pricing and value pricing as opposed to the dreaded billable hour.

3. Look at all your current service offerings and rank them by revenue. Are there profitable ones you could bundle?

4. Practice the value conversation with a client and prospect.

5. For your next prospect, offer at least three options to them based on the format addressed above. Judge the results and adjust.

Interviews to Go Deeper

1. How to Implement Value Pricing - with Ron Baker (https://jetpackworkflow.com/how-to-implement-value-pricing-with-ron-baker/)

2. Move to Value Based Billing - with Jason Blumer (https://jetpackworkflow.com/value-based-billing-paperless-flat-cpa-firm-jason-blumer/)

3. Add 19% to Bottom Line with Value Pricing - with Steve Major (https://jetpackworkflow.com/value-pricing-adds-profit-ditch-timesheets/)

4. Price on Value and Measure Success - Kirk Bowman (https://jetpackworkflow.com/art-value-interview-kirk-bowman/)

Recommendations

I interview firm owners every week and this is a hot button topic that continues to creep up. I've heard many ideas I couldn't flesh out further here. If your firm is contemplating changing up how you price, I invite you to reach out and we can chat about it.

Email me: david@jetpackworkflow.com

Chapter 3

Driving Growth in Your Firm

Special offer at end of chapter

Terry kick started his firm in Michigan and immediately got clients. Nothing magical, he started his career as a partner at a large firm. When he left to hang out his shingle, loyal clients followed along with a great network.

Starting a business wasn't what he had expected. At his old large firm, he was making a healthy six-figure plus bonus annual take-home. Suddenly, he's juggling more and more. After his first year, he began hiring as his clients would refer their friends every so often. He was growing organically.

Terry had never been the salesman type or a marketing man. Clients had just shown up from referrals at the beginning and it had worked. He bragged about how he "didn't need to market" to his friends. Then, without warning, the referrals stopped. Everything slowed down.

The wealth of new referrals dried up, growth slowed, and Terry had no idea why. Who knows why referrals come and go at all?

Frantically, he started attending networking events, desperate for new clients as he was still hiring to keep up with growth. He didn't want to fire anyone, but nothing seemed to work. A few ads in the local paper brought a couple of "cheap" wins, but that was it. *What had happened?*

Well, accountants are typically not the best marketers. I went into accounting because I loved numbers, but also because I *hated* selling. I thought I would never need to sell if I was an accountant.

My first experience with selling was in middle school. To raise money for a weekend retreat, we were given Vidalia onions to sell. Supposedly, moms would eat those up. Other kids sold cookies and chocolate, and we had onions.

Many of my friends went door to door in their neighborhood selling the smelly bags. Some sold 10, another sold around 20. But not me. I was terrified of selling. I had a limiting belief that sales is slimy. It was always there in the back of my mind, so in the end, I sold just two.

And guess who bought them.

Not my parents. Me. I dipped into my dinky allowance jar and pulled out $30 just to claim I had sold two stinky bags.

Generally, other accountants have a similar viewpoint. They feel sales is slimy and you need to be pushy, manipulative, and a kiss-up; a stereotypical used car salesman. In all actuality, those are myths and limiting beliefs we hold on to because we're hoping to avoid selling.

I know because I was the same way. I took my first accounting job as a financial analyst. A handful of friends I graduated with went on to be salesmen for different companies or in retail sales positions.

"Lucky I'm not them…"

When I left accounting to work for myself, helping financial companies get more clients, I had to jump into the pool of sales. Here's what I learned: it all comes down to how you view yourself and what you offer.

A sale should be about *helping* another person. There are businesses in your area that stress out about their financial situation. If you lay out exactly the steps your firm can take to get their financial situation resolved, you are doing a service. The prospect will thank you again and again.

And in the process, you made a sale. It wasn't a *slimy* exchange. You went in confident about how you could help, and the prospect listened and realized you were the ticket to a healthier business.

That's where marketing shows its power.

Firms and partners get in their own way because of what's going on in between their ears. If you're 400% confident that what you do will help a business, making the sale is just the bridge between someone in need and someone who will help them.

In the past, to capture new clients, firms would rely on word-of-mouth referrals, networking events, and even print ads, as Terry had. These are still viable ways to get clients and I will touch on these later in this chapter. However, with the dawn of the Internet, it has become much easier for you to get in front of new clients. This means you can spend less time prospecting and more time shaking hands and onboarding.

As we mentioned in Chapter 1, partners of the firm should be spending 50–70% of their time looking for new clients. This will fluctuate depending on the firm and how it's structured, but your time is much too valuable to be spent solely on compliance work. Your expertise and personal brand is much more useful in front of new clients.

Firms owners, like Terry, love bragging about not having to market. *"We haven't had to spend $1 on marketing in years,"* they boast. But running your business on "referrals only" is NOT a badge of honor.

It can be dangerous for growth. All this statement means is you aren't willing to risk a little money to get more of the clients you want.

The largest companies in the world—Apple, Google, McDonald's—they all still advertise and spend billions of dollars annually. Apple has tens of billions in cash just sitting in their bank account and they still market themselves. They advertise to bring in more of the customers they want, and you should be doing the same.

Relying on only referrals means you aren't in control. Referrals are unpredictable. On top of that, you don't know what types of referrals you get. One firm I chatted with had bought a conference booth twice a year, but other than that they had so many referrals, they thought they didn't need to do any more marketing. The problem was the referrals were all small accounts.

They had a handful of big clients who made up a large portion of their annual revenue. Yet, all that came in the door were small $1,500-a-year clients. They weren't out there trying to snag the big client. On top of that, their workflow and processes weren't in tip-top shape, so new goldfish-size clients just added more work on top of the already shaky foundation.

This is why it is key to go through Chapter 1 first, before even thinking about new clients. Building on a shaky foundation will only make problems worse, but once you've taken care of that, allowing referrals to be your only marketing "tactic" removes your power in the market and allows other firms to snap up those valuable clients.

Benefits of Sales & Marketing:

- You attract more of the clients you actually want.
- Your firm grows at a faster, more predictable pace.

- Your staff is more excited about the projects they get to work on.
- You learn an invaluable skill for your life, even outside work.

To sell and market effectively, you must first know who your target market is and the messaging that will draw them in. You will create an "avatar" of what a perfect client looks like for both you and your team. When you do this, you'll better understand your target client and you'll know how to position your marketing and outreach campaigns. When a prospect feels you understand them and their industry, they are much more open to a conversation.

First, you'll want to pick up actual strategies you can implement right away to attract these ideal clients. Then, once they are in the door, you'll need to know what to *say* to get the prospect to sign on the dotted line. In this chapter, you will get a crash course in selling.

Before diving in, there's always the question of who should be handling the marketing in your firm. To be honest, marketing is a full-time responsibility. The top CPA firms have a dedicated marketing department. Maybe you can't have an entire department, but you should have at least one person dedicated to the craft of marketing and sales.

I don't mean a hybrid, though. You do not want a CPA who also dabbles in marketing. You need a full-time person who is in the weeds everyday trying to market your firm and support the partners in their business development efforts.

I work with many financial companies and that's exactly what they do. On top of that, they hire me to help with the workload and contribute outside ideas and perspectives. Someone who isn't in battle everyday with you will see a different picture. Much like the saying, *"Seeing the forest for the trees."*

Hiring someone may take a little bit of time, but it is essential for having the most productive marketing in your area.

Buckle up and get ready to fuel your marketing and double your firm!

Market and Messaging

Before getting into the more "sexy" talk about tactics and selling, you must set the foundation. Much like you must have a solid foundation with your workflow and processes before bringing on more clients, you need to establish the foundation of your marketing and sales processes by understanding your market and developing your messaging.

Your "market" answers the question, *"Who do I serve?"* This could be broad, such as "any person or business within 20 miles of my location," or specific, such as, "we're focused on bookkeeping and accounting services for construction companies in Pennsylvania."

Generally, the more specific your market, the better.

Your "message" is your *Unique Selling Proposition* (USP). It answers the question, *"Why should I do business with you instead of another firm?"*

Every day, you are bombarded with thousands of advertisements. We've become numb to them over the years, so your message needs to cut through the clutter and resonate with your target market. To do this, it boils down a powerful USP.

Think about the first time you bought a house. You could throw a rock and hit a realtor every time because there are millions of them everywhere. If you didn't know anyone in the area, how did you know which realtor to give your business to?

All of them have "homebuyers" as a market and *all* of them shout their message, "We'll get you the best deal," and, "We work harder for you." The canned lines are endless.

So, who do you pick?

Now, imagine a new realtor rolled into town. Realtor M&M. He takes out an ad in the paper:

> *Looking to buy your first home? Dozens of families in your city just closed on their first homes. To get your free guide on the secrets to buying your first home and not getting ripped off by realtors, call this number.*

Suddenly, all the canned lines from before sound even worse. Realtor M&M understands you and he specializes in first-time home buying. At least you think he does.

You are going to call Realtor M&M, even though you could find a realtor every five feet. You can find a new CPA firm every 20 feet, so you must differentiate your market and messaging to attract clients and convince them to work with you instead of with your many competitors. It's just a matter of untangling it and putting pen to paper.

Your Market

When I tell owners to hone in on their market, they immediately worry about missing out on potential clients. It sounds like you're excluding potential business when you narrow down your market, but as you build a firm, you want as much predictability as possible because predictability equals efficiency, and efficiency equals more profit.

Take one firm who only has dentists as clients. Well, all the CPAs understand the industry fully. The process for one dentist will mirror another fairly closely and replication of the process and workflow increases capacity. The CPAs get faster at the work they do and the firm can charge more because of their "expert" status in the dental industry.

Take another firm who has clients in multiple industries. Different industries require different knowledge, so their CPAs need to study various tax implications for each industry. General knowledge of the industry means less expertise to pass on to a client. It takes them more time to do their job, plus they could never have all the knowledge they need to serve clients in one industry perfectly. Less expertise equals less efficiency, which equals lower profits.

I'm not recommending you throw out all clients from other industries, but what I want you to realize is that the most profitable firms operate like an assembly line. Car companies make billions by taking a few models of a car and replicating it over and over and over again. When you specialize in your market, you can do the same.

Now, you still might be thinking this is counterintuitive. By narrowing your market you will, by definition, *decrease your market size*. But that is not necessarily a bad thing. Some of the upsides are:

- You can craft specific services to meet their specific needs.
- You can craft a specific message that speaks to that particular market—think of Realtor M&M.
- You will spend marketing dollars where you *know* the client is—on or offline.

Many new firms and even some more experienced ones have the idea that they want to serve whoever is willing to pay them. Their market it essentially everyone. When you are starting out and need to keep the lights on, this makes sense, but as you grow, a one-size-fits-all structure damages your marketing budget and won't bring in the best clients.

If you target everyone in the world, where do you spend your marketing dollars? Your options include:

- Local radio
- Every local paper
- Business journals
- Conferences
- Direct mail
- Social media

And the list goes on. You don't know where your target market hangs out, so you throw money against the wall and wait for something to stick. Remember, we live in the knowledge economy and your expertise is more valuable than ever. Clients will open their wallets over and over for specialists. The heart surgeon's paycheck dwarfs the generalist's because heart surgery is a valuable expertise.

If you transformed into the "Dental CPA," dentists would line up and shell out more money to work with you than with the "General CPA." They perceive you as more valuable because you understand their problems and their industry. With your target market, you will want a nice mix of clients who all won't balk at paying your prices, so providing as high of a perceived value as possible is key.

Although you have a target market, you can still serve clients in various industries. However, you benefit most when you are *known* as a specialist in a certain area. Realtor M&M is *known* as a specialist in first-time homebuyers, but he also cashes commission checks from selling houses and buying luxury properties.

It's easy to say what you should do, but how can you actually do it? How should you start narrowing your market and finding a niche?

Here are some questions to consider:

- Who is happy to pay the most for your expertise and services?
- Who do you enjoy working with?
- Who are you in position to serve best?
- Who is under- or poorly served?

You want to answer these questions with specifics. If your answer to all the above is "all business owners," you're being too broad. It should feel uncomfortable narrowing down your market.

When answering these questions, you want to focus on a specific industry or a specific type of business. Let's say you reevaluate the questions and decide that because you have a strong core group of clients in the construction industry, you decide to look into defining that as your core market. And because you want owners that are well established, you want construction companies that have at least $1 million in revenue.

Great, we're off to a creating a solid marketing foundation. Once you focus on a single market, it's time to create a **client avatar**.

Client Empathy Map

We have a target market—construction companies doing at least $1M in revenue—so, we can create a profile of who we want to market to.

This might feel a bit silly, but you'd be amazed at what comes out of this exercise. You will start to understand what makes your clients tick, which helps you position your firm better, create better marketing, and even assist in defining additional services you'd like to offer.

For this exercise, I prefer to use a **client empathy map**, which you can see below. This is my preferred technique because it forces us to walk a mile in our market's shoes.

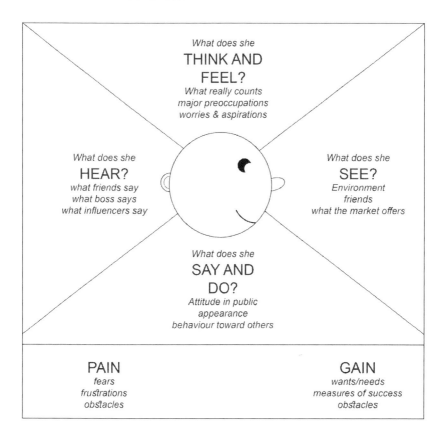

The goal of the exercise is to get a 360° view of your target client, what they see and hear in terms of their influences, and what their fears and obstacles are. When you understand a specific market perfectly, you will find many similarities between all the individuals in the market and you can address their problems directly. When you know all of this, you can talk to a group of your ideal clients collectively while also speaking to them on an individual basis. We will dive into this as we go.

Nothing in marketing starts perfect, so don't be overwhelmed in thinking this exercise needs to provide a perfect, bulletproof avatar. Simply thinking through some of these questions will open the doors to profitable marketing.

And notice how we haven't even touched tactics like social media, email, direct mail, or anything. This foundation is something that transcends the latest shiny object and will stand the test of time.

Where can you start finding information about your ideal clients?

- Trade magazines
- Websites around the niche
- Talking with professionals in the industry
- Books (free at the library)
- Facebook and Linkedin groups
- Documentaries and shows on cable and Netflix

These are just a few of the places you can start. You will begin to see some trends.

So as we go through the empathy map, perhaps we find:

- Many top trade magazines for construction owners talk about how accounts receivables and cash flow kill the profits of many companies. (This falls under Hear)
- Many owners started their business with a sense of pride because they were so good at their trade, but have since distanced themselves from the daily work and have a hard time managing staff, operations, and everything else that goes on in the business. (Feel)
- Many owners spend their free time in the outdoors, and you actually see many outdoor ads in their trade magazines. (Say and Do)

- Their biggest fear is losing their company, or being absent from their family. (Pain)
- Their dream business is one where he/she can focus on talking with clients about their projects. (Gain)

The more you think through each section, not only does it improve your marketing, but it improves your client relationships. You've taken a huge step in internalizing your market's everyday experience, which informs the interactions you have with existing and potential clients.

Now that you understand your market, let's look at crafting the ultimate message or Unique Selling Proposition for them.

Your Message

As a copywriter and marketer, I believe that you might be able to narrow the right market down to the individual, but if the message is off, everything is ruined. Having an impactful USP helps you attract the right clients.

Your USP spotlights what you do differently and better than your nearby competitors. Think first about your market, *"What do you do for this market that they value and why do they want to work with you rather than another firm?"*

This is a loaded question. It's tempting to put down *all* your services, but you don't want to put down *what* you do. Instead, you want to describe *why* they want or need that service. What is the result for them when they work with you?

That's what clients pay for. Think back to Chapter 2: clients don't want to pay for your time; they want to pay for your expertise and the outcomes you can provide faster and better than others.

Nate Hagerty, marketing expert and owner of Tax Pro Marketer, remarks:

> *"When you implement a USP, as a firm, you are finally able to differentiate yourself from the rest of the competition clearly and concisely. You become attractive to your ideal client base, who doesn't want that?"*

Nate sees the problems many firms have when they sift through hundreds of marketing strategies from online gurus. He believes if you nail down the USP, you will know exactly which strategies to use.

Let's look at the equation for a client-attracting USP:

> *"We help X, do Y, so that they can get Z."*

For example, *we help seven- and eight-figure construction companies automate their back office finances, so they can they increase cash flow, grow faster, and save more money on their returns.*

Most firms stop at, "We help X, do Y." On top of that, their "X" usually boils down to "everyone." Notice, from the example, how specific it is. Again, this is the messaging we want in our marketing. Other companies, such as those in the medical and manufacturing industries will still find you and want to work with you, but you want as many of your ideal clients as possible.

Having more ideal clients allows you the option to cut out bad clients in some places because bad clients can hurt a firm in all places. To make it easier, let's look at another equation:

> *"Get X, under Y time frame, guaranteed."*

For example:

- Learn how top construction companies save over $10,000 on their returns, in under 30 minutes, guaranteed.
- We help top construction companies increase cash flow by 154% in under 30 days, guaranteed.

Now, construction owner ears are going to perk up. "Save over $10,000?" "Increase cash flow by 154%?" When you understand the industry, you know what the regular struggles are of owners. Then, you use a bit of psychology to get them curious about your firm.

Now, while these formulas may seem simple, finding the true benefit of your service can be challenging. To help kick start the process of thinking, writing, and speaking in benefits, fill out the Feature-Pain-Benefit grid below.

Use the formula: We do X so you can _____

The Feature Pain Benefit Grid

Feature	Pain	Benefit
We send you weekly cashflow reports	Missing critical financial information and being less profitable	Have complete transparency, each week, whether you're on track or decreasing profitability

---

This chart will help you think through the features and benefits that will be most attractive to your target market. Use the phrase, "So you can…" at the end of each service you offer to force the benefit out.

Once you've completed the grid, you will have a huge advantage over your competition, in that you will understand why your clients choose a specific service. By overlaying this feature-benefit analysis, you can then determine your USP with a service or statement that matches your target market.

Remember, you will know your target market when you answer these questions:

- Who is happy to pay the most for your expertise and services?
- Who do you enjoy working with?
- Who are you in position to serve best?
- Who is under- or poorly served?

Actual Strategies to Bring in New Clients

You might have been tempted to skip down to this section. Everyone loves to indulge in new tactics and strategies for growing a business but, the bus screeches to a halt there.

"Experts" churn out dozens of social media posts every single day about growing your firm and firm owners like yourself eat them up. So, the "experts" continue to pump them out onto the Internet.

There aren't that many *new, sexy* strategies in all these blogs. You probably see the same ideas over and over again. The ideas and tactics get parroted because firm owners read them, then do nothing.

We could have done the same thing with this entire section, but, we wanted to create something much better. If you follow these steps, one-by-one, we guarantee you will grow your firm this year.

Don't treat this as just another "article you just read." Treat it like your personal road map. These strategies transform regular firms who blend in with the competition into leaders in their markets.

All of these strategies require a great support system—your team—plus an effective workflow and process strategy. The strategies you're about to read won't be like blog posts you've read. Instead, these strategies will give specific direction on the most effective ways to execute them, based on our expertise and the top-notch professionals we talk with every day.

Reining in new clients sounds uncomfortable, but you will see how easy it can be when you apply the correct systems.

Inbound Marketing

First, let's define inbound marketing and compare it to outbound options.

Inbound marketing means using certain marketing tactics that *pull* prospects to you. Some examples are books, blogs, podcasts, videos, networking, and referrals. Inbound will normally involve content and information of some sort. In our case, this book gives us social proof in the CPA and accounting world. Now, a firm owner might read this and reach out to hire us because they trust us and they know we know what we're talking about.

Inbound marketing circulates trust of your firm's brand and of yourself as a professional.

Outbound marketing, then, means using certain marketing tactics that *push* your products and services upon a prospect. Some examples include cold calls, print advertisements, direct mail, and face-to-face selling. Much of outbound marketing revolves around contacting people you don't know to drum up business. While outbound marketing proves to bring in new clients faster, tactics like cold calling can be discouraging.

We recommend a mix of both inbound and outbound strategies. At Jetpack, every week we put out content and podcasts to help firm owners run a better, more profitable practice. Later in this chapter, you will learn a successful outbound strategy that doesn't cost thousands.

For now, let's focus on inbound strategies.

When it comes to determining the best strategies for your business, start with your market and message. *Consider where your clients like to consume information and the type of media they consume. Do they listen to podcast shows, read blog posts, skim infographics?*

At Jetpack, we utilize blogs and a podcasts. Other firms tap into YouTube. There are multiple opportunities you can take advantage of.

If we look back at our construction CPA firm, we concluded: construction owners enjoy listening to quick, 15-minute shows for both information and entertainment value. They subscribe to various publications and frequently Google financial regulations that are frequently changing.

From this information, we can come up with a few options for inbound marketing:

- Developing a weekly 15-minute podcast for construction owners.

- Adding a blog that targets financial regulations for construction firm owners.
- Submitting content to the top construction publications.
- Packaging an e-book together to help your clients.

Podcasts

At Jetpack, our podcast, the Grow Your Firm Podcast (https:// jetpackworkflow.com/category/growing-your-firm-podcast/), attracts regular prospects. They listen to the show, enjoy it, learn from it, and contact the team. Many of our guests are also subscribers to our Jetpack Workflow software (https://jetpackworkflow.com/).

Launching a podcast takes some preparation. While blogging simply requires opening up a "new post" page and typing away, podcasting requires a bit of technological know-how, being (or at least acting) comfortable in front of a microphone, and finding guests in interview, plus hosting and equipment fees.

I'm not going to spend pages going through the steps to getting your podcast going. Instead, I'll refer you to this video to walk you through the steps:

>>> **Video with Step-by-Step instructions to getting your podcast up available at https://www.youtube.com/watch?v=xu2QNUY5iyk** <<<

Both of us have hosted podcasts and have been guests on shows, so we understand what makes an interesting, newsworthy show, and which ones are headed to mediocrity. To avoid mediocrity, here are our best tips for having an interesting show and how to be a great host:

- **Focus each episode on a theme:** It's tempting to get the microphone in front of you and start jabbering away, but that's not going to help your listeners. Instead, outline the topics you want to cover. If you have a guest, nudge them along a theme, especially if they are an expert in a certain area. Shows are less interesting when they are all over the map. When listeners want to learn, keep it focused.

- **Ask the questions your audience cares about:** Approach your themes thinking, "What are the main questions a new audience member might have about this topic?" Ask your guest these questions. Don't throw softballs. Instead, think of them as your personal consultant.

- **Have energy:** Even if you aren't a naturally energetic person, you must inject excitement into your voice. It helps keep your listeners engaged and projects confidence and knowledge of a subject.

Podcasts can have massive benefits for your Firm's brand:

- You gain exposure to new audiences outside of your area.
- Your personal brand grows, which separates you from competitors.
- It could lead to speaking engagements.
- It grants credibility to your firm.

One major point—again, a podcast can be tough to get going. There's a learning curve, plus you might not see the fruit of your work for many months, or even a year. You will start off with a small listener base. All shows do, unless backed or started by a celebrity. So, *patience is key*.

Written Content

Another inbound marketing strategy you can implement is written content: an e-book, a blog, or posts on other websites.

Edward Mendlowitz, Parter at WithumSmith + Brown, advises creating content targeted at "specific" groups of your clients. He creates a series of posts and then personally emails them to his clients, letting them know he thought of them. This allows your posts to get out there and circulated while also making your clients feel like all-stars.

Your first instinct when thinking about writing content might be: *"I'm not a writer."* Let me dispel this: when you read informative posts, you want the information, not a perfectly written piece. You aren't trying to get published in the *New York Times*. Your clients don't care, as long as there is value in what you've written.

When you sit down to write the next great American novel, you can worry about your writing chops. Now, all you need is expertise.

Well, first you need an idea. To find an appropriate topic, refer back to the client empathy map and tap into the various pain points of your target market. For construction owners, it might be cash flow, so an idea germinates:

3 Places to Find More Cash Flow for Your Construction Business

A hotel owner *might* read that. A construction owner will *definitely* read it. See why your messaging and understanding your market is important?

You, being a financial expert, have knowledge your client base would love to extract. You want to offer your experience up to attract clients. Now, you might be thinking, *why would they now pay me if I give the ideas away for free?*

But that is exactly the answer: ideas are just ideas. Everyone has new ideas, but execution is what separates the winners and losers. Potential clients will see your blog and respect your experience, but they still need someone to make it happen. Your clients pay for results, not your ideas.

For example, this book gives you a vault of the best strategies for firm owners and you're paying virtually nothing. That's great for you, but now you might want to implement these right away and need help. Your first thought would probably be to call us. If not, it's not a big deal, but inbound marketing is a *pull* strategy, so it offers potential clients evidence of our expertise with opportunities to reach out to us and become clients.

By now, you have an idea of what you could write about. It can be a simple thought or an extensive media strategy. Whatever it is, write down all your ideas as they come. Open an Evernote account and flesh them out. You'll find ideas appear at random moments: in the shower, while you are skiing, during a random conversation, so having an accessible way to make notes will help.

A typical blog post shouldn't go over 1,000 words, in most cases. An ebook can run as long or short as you would like.

Before you start writing, outline the points you want to make. Write down your main pieces of advice or arguments, any stories you wish to include, resources you can refer to, etc. Now, just start writing.

Here's a secret for any writing—the best writing comes from the editing. After you finish writing the first draft, step away from it for a day or so. Forget about it. Then, come back to it and start editing. What happens is your subconscious works out more of the post while you aren't focusing on it. New ideas will come up, better phrasing of certain points, a new story. Now, you're ready to go.

You will only get better at writing as you do more of it, there are no shortcuts to it, but here are my top three quick tips for better writing:

1. If you can, include compelling stories that evoke emotion.
2. Avoid, at all costs, business jargon. It doesn't make you don't look smarter.
3. Use a free app such as the Hemingway Editor (http://www.hemingwayapp.com/), to dissect your writing

I know creating content no one reads can be exhausting and discouraging. Remember, it takes time. To shorten the timeframe to new clients, consider these steps:

1. Email your clients when you publish a new post.
2. Refer to people in your posts and ask them to share it with their audience.
3. Make it easy to share with social media share buttons.
4. Post it to your company's social media and your personal page.
5. Put together a list of potential readers and email them directly to tell them about how your blog might help.
6. Get your content picked up by another website.

BONUS:

Reaching out to publications or newspapers is an effective strategy for reaching new audiences, but it can be intimidating. Here's a script you can use to ask a publisher to use your work:

Dear Publisher,

I see many construction owners in your audience and believe I could add some value.

My Firm, X, specializes in helping construction owners grow their company with cash flow and tax strategies. Construction clients all struggle with juggling their cash flow with their various projects. Your readers might like this new post on finding more cash flow in their business.

Here's the post: [INSERT LINK]. It could fill an article slot on your site, especially if you're looking for new content to fill in the gaps. If it's easier to send as a Word doc or PDF, let me know.

Thanks, talk soon,

Name, Firm

LinkedIn

Jody Padar, CEO and Principal at New Vision CPA Group, constantly grows her Firm using social media. She sees so many Firms who treat social media as a boardroom meeting—very stuffy and full of business jargon.

She recommends being authentic and transparent with your social efforts. She says, *"Let your personality shine through on social media."*

Clients don't do business with faceless, boring corporations. They do business with people.

The dawn of the Internet opened the floodgates for every size company to do business online. A golden tool for professionals, Linkedin, leverages both your time and resources to get in front of the right person much faster.

If you're not familiar with it, LinkedIn is the social network for professionals. You can scroll through company listings, find the CFO, the CEO, the administrative assistant of any business and you save precious time calling around looking for the owner or for their email.

Professionals go on LinkedIn *expecting* to talk and read about business. This gives you a tremendous advantage as your client already "walks in" with the mindset you need. So many firms have no clue about how to get clients with LinkedIn, so this could be the "magic pill" you've been looking for.

The good news is, tapping into LinkedIn grows steadily but hasn't peaked yet as a major prospecting tool. *In this section, I will walk you through the steps to finding the right people and getting the meeting,* whether you have years of sales experience or none at all.

Most professionals and executives will have a profile set up, but that's where everything stops. They treat it as a place to show off your resume.

But you know better. LinkedIn opens doors because the initial "awkward" stage goes out the window. If someone cold calls you, you know nothing about them and don't trust them. If you see someone on LinkedIn, it lowers your guard because you can browse through their profile, find some similarities, and see their picture.

This section will cover:

1. Setting up your LinkedIn profile
2. Finding your ideal clients
3. Reaching out to your ideal clients
4. Following up with your prospects

Setting Up Your Profile

As previously mentioned, your profile shouldn't be about showing off your resume. LinkedIn is your sales tool, so it needs to attract your clients and compel them to pick up the phone and chat with you.

To save time, I will assume you already have a LinkedIn profile, and you have added a nice, professional profile picture and filled in details about your current and past work. Those basics can be done in 1–2 hours. Do not worry about signing up for premium services at the moment, so leave that be.

With this strategy, your profile acts as the foundation for everything. Much like workflow and processes act as the foundation for your firm, your LinkedIn profile must be done properly before the other tactics come into play.

I recommend starting at the bottom of your profile. Fill in various activities and volunteer work you do and add skills. Profile-viewers browse through these sections the least. You should include keywords for your demographics: "Construction accounting," "Taxes for construction owners," etc.

You can put these under Activities as it registers as a keyword when others search for you, but it doesn't appear in a spot most people read. You want to build from the bottom up simply to get your writing mindset going. For many accountants, talking about yourself is uncomfortable. Get that out of your system in the lower portions.

Working your way up to your job descriptions, I recommend keeping past job descriptions very short. Unless you did something incredible at these positions, make these descriptions no more than one or two lines. If you won an award, throw that in.

Less is more in this case. You want to save all your creative juices for your current position. When you write your current position's description, follow these steps:

1. Include your position at the top.

2. Make sure your firm's name is correct and links to the Company Page. If there isn't one for your firm, discuss this with marketing.

3. First sentence: Explain your *"We help X, do Y, so that they can get Z"*

4. Second sentence: Include a short list of notable clients. You can be vague if you aren't allowed to disclose that information.

5. Next ten sentences: Talk directly to your ideal clients. You should know your market and your message well enough to understand what an ideal prospect goes through each day.

Let's look at an example. I work with firms and advisors to help find them more clients. Here's what my "current position" looks like on LinkedIn:

You might think networking events + "organic" referrals are the only way to grow your business. Look, those things are awesome, but you end up:

1. Not working with the exact clients you want

2. You are not IN CONTROL of your lead generation.

What if you could spend the time doing what you wanted to do when you signed up in this industry: servicing, consulting, helping those who need your financial expertise?

Instead, you spend countless hours prospecting, hitting the phones, having awkward "salesy" conversations with random strangers you meet at events.

Forget all that.

You simply need a plan:

I build that marketing plan for you. Because we're a small company, you aren't paying bloated fees the "full service" (aka jack of all trades) marketing company will charge you. You won't be paying for my morning bagels or my over-the-top office, just:

- More clients you love

- More profit

- More work/life balance

How does that sound?

Having better copy & digital marketing strategies makes lead generation THAT much easier to grow your firm.

See how simply it is written? No business jargon or droning about "Here are all the services we offer." In accounting, most business owners don't understand half of the compliance work you do. They probably aren't looking on LinkedIn to find a "real estate tax compliant audit partner." This is why your benefit statement is so essential.

Now, this will take some time to flesh out. Show it to your spouse and your fellow partners. It needs to be compliant with any SEC regulations, but that's much easier to do than you think.

Moving up, you are now at the Summary section. This is the second piece LinkedIn browsers will read after your headline, so it is critical to get right.

Your Summary must touch on the absolute, most important pain points and benefits you provide. Your job title is a nice sidekick to your Summary, but your Summary hammers home the main points.

1. First sentence: Start with an *"If you…"* sentence. It touches on the biggest pain you can solve for your ideal client.

   "If you're a construction owner and you never seem to have enough cash at the end of the month, you have a cash flow and tax management problem."

2. Second sentence: Dig into the pain even more.

   "Going into debt and missing payroll is a recipe for a bankrupt business."

3. Third sentence: Start going into your services to appease this pain:

   a. *"Provide tax planning strategies that have saved clients 30% more than average."*

   b. *"Cash flow management consulting so you have the money you need at the end of the month, plus, a little extra to take home."*

4. Rest of Summary: Discuss *why* you do this.

   "I've spent 20 years working with construction owners, seeing the day-in, day-out stress of handling multiple projects and their finances. There just aren't many great resources or advisors out there for you. I'm building my career by helping you build your company."

This Summary should directly key in who your target client is. This is a great time to remind you: you *are not* trying to get every business owner as a client. You want the best, most profitable clients for your firm.

You will still get prospects from outside the industry, do not worry about that. But you need the right bait for the right type of clients.

The beauty of all this is, if you want to move on to targeting another industry, you can update your profile in a day. I'm stressing this because you probably feel a bit squeamish about targeting just one type of company.

You're probably thinking, *"But I'm leaving money on the table."*

No, you're not. Remember that specialists get paid more and are respected more. That's what we are doing here.

Now, let's move on to the final piece: your headline. Perhaps the most crucial piece of your profile and you only have about 90 characters to get everything in.

Most partners have this as their headline: *Partner at X Firm.*

That tells people *nothing* about yourself, your business, or your clients. It is very self-focused. Instead, you want to use your messaging as the focal point:

> *I help construction co. increase cash flow & save money*
> *on taxes by automating your finances*

See how this is client-focused? Use the "I help X…" template and you will get more profile views and interested parties reaching out to you.

At this point, you want to go back through your profile and fill in where you need to. Editing is essential to great writing and a great profile needs *great writing*.

Only after doing this step should you start moving forward.

Finding Your Ideal Clients

Earlier, we discussed thinking about where your clients hang out. They might be reading certain publications, visiting specific websites, or joining specific groups. On LinkedIn, you simply want to find somewhere a collection of them might congregate.

The best place for this is find LinkedIn Groups.

LinkedIn Groups grant access to members and allow them to partake in discussions about the topic or theme of that group. For example, if you are a CPA in New York, there might be a group called New York CPAs. If you request to join and look around, you will most likely see fellow CPAs from the area.

You don't want to join where your *competitors* are. Instead, you need to locate where your *ideal clients* will be.

First, find any 1st degree connections (people you already are connected with) who fit your ideal client profile. Scroll down and see which groups they are in. Request to join those groups.

Second, go to the "Groups" page, where you manage the groups you're in. Start searching using the keywords your client would use. For example, *"Construction owners," "Builders,"* etc. Find these general groups and start requesting to join.

Then, go through the member list of these groups looking for clients who fit your ideal profile. Check out their profiles and scroll down to see which groups they are involved in. You can join up to 50 groups at a time.

> **Note:** *You can only request to join a small number of groups at a time. Wait to be given access. If after two weeks you haven't gotten in, withdraw your request and find another group.*

In my opinion, spending a ton of time in groups never had much benefit to me as most groups are simply filled with random postings by members. Not much interaction occurs thus it's best not to spend too much time going through them. All you want is the list of members IN the group.

This portion can take some time as you get used to using LinkedIn. You will get the hang of it, so just keep joining groups and finding new ones to join.

Another way to find ideal clients is to go back to profiles of an ideal client, scroll down, and peek at the "People Also Viewed" section. Many business owners hang out with other business owners. About ten names are listed there for you to scrape and add to your ideal client list.

Finally, do an advanced search and start putting keywords in. You can filter by location, company size, industry, and more.

> *Note: As you use LinkedIn more, Advanced Search gets blocked will be blocked. Once you get up to speed and ready to do more with LinkedIn, invest in the monthly Business Plus plan. It unlocks much more in terms of features and access.*

Reaching Out to Your Ideal Client

By now, you should have access to a handful of groups. This is the moment of truth.

Your goal is to reach out to 10–15 new potential connections every day of the week. Obviously, not everyone is going to connect with you; however, a percentage of those who do connect will then say "yes" to getting on a call with you.

From my own prospecting, you should see a 40–60% acceptance rate of invitations. Then, 25% of the accepted will agree to further the conversation. Of that group, 5-15% will become clients.

Here's the math:

- 10-15 connection requests each day = 70 requests per week.
- If 50% accept, that's 35 new connections per week.

- Then, 25% agree to a phone call, which is 9 new calls per week
- **About 5-15% will become clients = 1 new client per week.**

As you get better at the process, your close rate will steadily increase. Remember, if you get just 60 clients a year, that is worth millions of dollars!

Prospecting on LinkedIn can be effective and useful. It just comes down to putting in the effort. This process takes some legwork, which is why you might want to get a team member to do this for you.

You should aim to spend no more than one hour a day on LinkedIn.

The steps to do this? Very simple, you have your list of groups you joined. Now, open up those groups and start going down the list of members.

Find the members you believe fall into your ideal client category and shoot them a connection request. You *do not* want to send a generic "Please connect with me," request. You want to personalize it as much as possible. Try something like this:

"Hi Jack,

I saw we shared a few connections and groups. Your background running X company really interested me as I'm in the same industry. I would love to hear more.

Let's connect here if you're open to it,

Thanks! Joe"

See how simple it is? You can copy and paste this for each request and change a few minor details. Let me breaking down what I do:

- First, I make sure to highlight how we are similar. People love to hang out with others who are like them.
- Second, I compliment his background and tell him how interesting it is.
- I end with asking for a connection and adding "if you are open to it."

This last line gives them the option to say no. See, if you send too many connection requests and the receiver says "I don't know this person," you will get blocked from being able to send requests.

I've found that when I add this last line, most will appreciate it and will simply "ignore" the request if they aren't interested. Having your request "ignored" doesn't go as a strike against you.

A reminder, as you go to each profile, make sure you peek over to the "People Also Viewed" column to easily find similar ideal prospects.

What makes this system work is its predictability. You can turn the faucet on and off as you need more clients. Say you get nine new connections on the phone and all nine become clients, you could take a break from prospecting for a few weeks. When you are ready to start again, just get back to sending out requests.

This is much like workflow. You want it to be predictable.

If someone doesn't accept your invitation, don't take it personally. Many people don't check LinkedIn all the time, plus, many executives get pounded with invitation requests and just don't accept any of them. Adding a personalized note increases your chances of getting accepted!

Try this out for a few months, you will be surprised at the results. But, before you do that, go through this next section as it's imperative for getting that initial call setup.

Follow Up with Your Prospects

The key to any successful salesperson lies *not* in the slick words they use, but in their follow up. You have to remember that business owners are not waiting anxiously for your sales pitch. They, like you, juggle various projects everyday. Sprinkle in stress and you'll realize you don't fit into their daily life.

A prospect could be interested in your work but it slips their mind. Perhaps they simply need a nudge in the right direction. *From you.*

Whether a prospect finds you organically, through networking, or from a call thanks to LinkedIn, you need to implement this right away to stay top of mind with your prospects. But *when should you follow-up?*

The answer? Anytime you interact with a prospect where the next logical step would move closer to a sale. The goals of following up should be:

- Get a "yes"
- Get a "no"

Getting a "maybe" ruins the point of following up because you are back to where you started: unsure if they are interested.

If someone keeps giving you a "maybe," it's best to simply confront them on it and push them to a "no." Customers always feel they are in control and are willing to toy with a salesman to see if they can get a better deal. Also, many people just don't like telling a salesman "no," especially if you've spent a good deal of time with them.

Let's first dig into regular follow-ups. You'll want to follow up with a prospect a minimum of for times. Getting about seven touch points is the ideal starting point.

Many new CPAs give up after one time because they don't want to be pushy. Following up isn't pushy when done strategically and through a system. Let me outline the follow-ups here:

1. Follow-ups can best be started through email. A simple email you can send:

    Dear Jane,

    Following up, I never heard back after our discussion. Does it make sense to set up a quick call to revisit a few of the issues you had managing cash flow?

    Let me know, thanks!

    Joe

    Note: It's very short. You aren't trying to re-sell them in one email. All you need to do is bring up the problems they had again so they can revisit the pain they feel.

2. After a week, follow up again.

    Dear Jane,

    I never heard back. How does your calendar look to discuss further?

    Thanks,
    Joe

    Note: Very simple. All you are trying to do is get them to think of you again. You can also include in the postscript a link to some relevant content they might find useful. It's even better if you wrote the content yourself. Tie it back into the issues they had before.

For example: *PS: Jane, here's a piece I wrote recently about finding an extra $10,000 in cash flow a month. Based on our initial chat, you might find it useful.*

3. After two weeks, follow up again.

   Dear Jane,

   I don't mean to be a pest, but I haven't heard back. Is this still an interest for you?

   Thanks,
   Joe

   Note: Again, very quick. You are laying the groundwork to get them to say "no." If it's not an interest to them, they will think that to themselves.

4. Then, you send the last email.

   Dear Jane,

   I haven't heard back. Usually when this happens, it means one of two things: You are very busy and this isn't a good time, or you're not interested.

   I won't follow-up after this: Should I close your file? Are we done here?

   Thanks,
   Joe

   Note: This is a gutsy email to send, but remember this: you lose *nothing* by getting a "no" from a client. It's easier for you, trust me, to know it's not happening than to carry a small, false hope there's a chance. Small hope prospects waste your energy and your time thinking about them or following up.

It's also a very direct statement and question: "Are we done here?" If you receive this, you would most likely feel compelled and bad for the salesmen. You are more likely to send a "no."

Typical Responses & Your Responses:

Getting a "Yes"

Your response: *"Great, let's set up a time to chat. How's Thursday at 2, 3, or 4?"*

Getting a "No."

Your response: *"Thanks for letting me know, Jane. Even though we aren't going to work together, I did want to provide value. Here's an ebook I wrote that goes over different solutions to some of the problems we discussed. If it's not a problem, I'll follow up in 6 months as I know many things can change. Thanks."*

Getting a "Wishy-Washy Answer"

Wishy-washy answers look like this:

- *"Can you give me a few weeks?"*
- *"We are still thinking it over, can you do [X] for us to make a better decision?"*
- *"I'm still talking to my partners."*
- *"We are still looking at the options."*
- *"I'll add you to our vendors list."*
- If they've rescheduled or pushed you off a few times already, this is a wishy-washy response.

These are answers you don't want. With these, you want to be very direct and dig into the heart of it. Here's how:

1. Reverse it:

   a. "What do you mean by 'give you a few weeks'? What's going on now?"

   b. "I don't understand, what else can I give you that would change your mind?"

   c. "What do you still need to discuss, what questions are left?"

   d. "What do you mean by 'looking at other options'? Usually this means you are close with a competitor. Should I close this file?"

   e. "When you say 'add to vendor list,' are you saying there isn't a need anytime soon? Should I close the file?"

   f. "Jane, we've kicked the can down the road a few times already. Usually, this means someone is just not interested. Should I close your file?"

2. Close the file.

   Remember, the purpose of following up is to get a "yes" or a "no." Cut "maybes" out of your pipeline so you can forget it and move on.

Completing these steps will help you grow and toughen up in many ways. You will feel accomplished with successful calls and quickly forget those who aren't interested. Business isn't personal.

Networking

A more "old school" tactic, networking lives at the top of the list for most partners prospecting for new clients. I bring it up here because you should put yourself out there a bit, but you need to network correctly so you aren't wasting your time.

When partners struggle again and again with networking, the problem is that they don't know which events to go to. For the most impactful networking, you don't want to go to just *any* event and give yourself a gold star for networking. Instead, you must be strategic about where you go and what you do there.

Remember, Chapter 1? Your time adds too much to the top-line to waste hours at fruitless networking events. Preparing your battle plan for your networking time can prove just as important as your preparation for workflow and business processes.

Let's take a quick look at the benefits of networking:

- Meeting new potential friends and partners.
- Giving yourself a nice diversion from your regular work pattern.
- Building your circle of influence.
- Improving your communication skills.
- Learning what other successful professionals are doing.

The main reason partners believe they should always be networking revolves around building your circle of influence. For those who don't know, think of it as a private dinner table. Sitting at the table are professionals from various industries, who intertwine regularly with your own work. For a CPA, it might include lawyers, financial advisors, bankers, financial software engineers, insurance professionals, management consultants, and even a client from your target market.

You would have one of each of these professionals in your circle and the code dictates, *if you have a referral for one of these industries, you send it to someone in your circle.* Then, everyone refers everyone to each other and there isn't any competition.

I've gone to countless networking events and I will say, most who go to these events have the same goal as you: more clients. These types of events advertise themselves as "business networking events," and the goal is to create new circles of influence out of thin air.

Drawing from my own experience, networking events like this can make developing a circle of influence challenging because you rarely know the other people very well, plus they don't tend to be consistent with their attendance. That means you aren't able to connect with new people, and you likely won't see most people from one event at another, so it's difficult to get to know anyone.

Your best chance at building a circle of influence begins with first looking through your own emails and phone calls. Ask yourself: *"Do I regularly talk with the same lawyer who represents a handful of my clients? Do many clients use the same bank and might they have an excellent banker they recommend?"*

The key is to find referrals to professionals already helping similar clients and who you know do their job well. You don't want to refer a client to an absolute stranger you stumbled on in the sandwich line at a networking event. You would be better off referring a client to someone who's proven to be trustworthy.

This brings us to the disadvantages of networking:

- There's a big risk of it being a waste of time.
- You typically won't run into the same people multiple times.
- It takes a long time for (good) referrals to generate from networking.
- Many who go to networking events are looking for clients as well.
- They can be uncomfortable, especially if you're an introvert.

To be blunt, if your firm needs clients *right now*, networking should be moved down the list of priorities. It takes months of effort with the same group before you see the fruits of your labor. While your firm grows steadily and you don't need a new client each week, networking, as a secondary strategy, plants the seeds for referrals down the line.

Up to now, you've read about where to begin compiling a list of candidates for your circle of influence. If you don't know other professionals through your own work, give your most trusted client a call and just ask. Explain what you're trying to do and the client will love you asked for their help.

I also explained how standard business events are a crap shoot, but that is not the case at all events. Some great places to find potential clients include:

- Industry conferences
- Workshops and seminars
- Awards dinners

When you go to industry conferences, choose ones where your ideal client would go. Eventbrite is a great way to find a list of events like this. It displays a chronological calendar of events, especially awards dinners, workshops and seminars.

You will probably not find new clients at the annual CPA conference. You want to go to industry conferences your client attends, like the annual construction firm conference. There, you mingle and learn more about the industry, and you're bound to run into owners who need your services.

"Ok, now what do I do and say at a networking event?"

Building Relationships at Events

Salesmen get a bad rap because they spend so much time talking. At least, that's the stereotype. Actually, the best salesmen listen more than they talk. A sale arises from uncovering a pain and solving it.

If you go to a networking event and just jabber the whole time, you will most likely turn people off from working with you. All they can imagine is being trapped on the phone as you chatter about things they don't care about.

The key to networking is to listen. With anyone new, spend 20% of the time talking and 80% listening and asking questions about them. Another great rule of thumb is: don't answer your own question after asking it.

For example:

> You: *"So, where are you from?"*
> Person: *"Colorado, I grew up near the mountains."*
> You: *"Cool, I grew up in California."*
> Person: *"Oh, great."*

This happens every day and it obliterates the conversation. Networking itself already feels uncomfortable. Rubbing elbows with strangers and mix in a dose of awkward conversation…No thanks.

Instead, push for the other person to talk more.

For example:

> You: *"So, where are you from?"*
> Person: *"Colorado, I grew up near the mountains."*
> You: *"Oh, that sounds fun. Did you get to ski much?"*
> Person: *"Actually yes, my Dad ran a small ski shop and I helped there every weekend."*
> You: *"Wow, so what got you into construction instead of working there?"*

See? Now you've got them chatting more. Everyone loves to talk about themselves. We all feel our life is more interesting than reality shows. As you dig into their past, you learn what they care about, their interests, why they do certain things. All of this information builds rapport and trust.

You'll find many will want to keep talking with you because of your conversation skills, even though, all you did was listen and ask questions!

To help you along, here are some sample questions you can ask to push the conversation further:

- *"What are the big issues you see everyday with what you do?"*
- *"What keeps you motivated?"*
- *"Tell me more about…"*

Again, networking can take months of digging and conversations before someone has the guts to refer a client to you.

Using the various strategies here: inbound marketing, LinkedIn, and networking, you will see new leads showing up at your door. At this stage, partners drop the ball. The limiting beliefs of feeling like a used car salesman causes blown sales.

That is why I put together a crash course on selling. I've taken the best of my knowledge and the wisdom from the guests on the podcast, and gift-wrapped it for you so you can skyrocket your close rate and bring in more revenue. You will find that in Chapter 4.

The Media

This hasn't been mentioned much yet because it's the least important piece. One of the biggest mistakes is to immediately jump to the *where* before thinking through the market or the message.

For example, we immediately jump onto Twitter to do online marketing, but is your market on there? Or we immediately want to advertise on radio, but does your market listen to that station?

Seth David, Founder and CEO of NerdEnterprises, realized his client base constantly asked him the same questions again and again. He knew they would be open to having an FAQ section that walks them through all the questions they might have.

After talking with many clients, he found blog posts were not the most effective way to share his answers and expertise. So, he turned to YouTube, a free platform to share and view videos on-demand. He's amassed millions of views because his clients constantly pull up the video site and watch his channel to find answers to their questions. This allows Seth to hone his message while also using a free medium to educate his clients and save himself time.

One of the most common mistakes when spending marketing dollars is investing in media without having a good grasp on your market or your message. If either the market or message is missing, it doesn't matter where you advertise.

If you don't know who your market is—or it's broadly defined as "people who need accounting work"—then you can justify advertising literally everywhere. And if you have a healthy six-figure marketing budget, go for it.

But if you're like most firms, your marketing dollars need to bring in an ROI within the next 30, 60 or 90 days. In that case, you can't afford to use the typical shotgun marketing approach, spraying ads everywhere in hopes that someone sees something.

So, we must define a market. One that has the ability to both utilize and pay for our services. And we have to craft a message, service, or offering that will serve them above and beyond the competition.

If we have those two things in place, we can then ask: *"Where does my market go to make purchasing decisions? Where do they go to get an informed opinion about something?"*

You can then list these media channels and begin building a list. For example, if we sell to construction companies, our list might include:

- Trade magazines they read.
- Websites or blogs they visit.
- Top authors or consultants in the space.
- Popular search terms for that industry.

Some of the media channels might be expensive, like ads in large publications, while others might be inexpensive or even free.

List as many as you can, and we can prioritize later. Once the list is created, the next step will be to put some numbers behind it. I cannot stress enough how important this process is.

With a full list of targeted media channels—try to get at least 10—you can then determine, based on price and expected return, which ones to try out first. Some will work, others will need to be tweaked, and some will get dropped completely. The point is that you have a targeted segment, a compelling message, and appropriate channels to test and measure.

Once you start measuring your marketing, you regain control of your budget, your growth, and your cash flow. For example, look at the sample data in this chart:

Media Marketing					
Name	**Website**	**Contact**	**E-mail/Phone**	**Cost**	**Expected ROI**
Bob's Construction Journal	bobsjournal.com	Bob Smith	Bob@bobsjournal.com 412-123-3124	$300/ month	Typical campaign brings in 200 views. Goal is 5 consultations and 2 Quickbooks sales.

When I contact a media channel, I want to know what the average views, clicks, or visitors a typical campaign can bring in. They might not give you a straight answer, but you should be able to get a typical or average response they've seen with a similar campaign in the past three months. They will have that information on file. Knowing this limits the risk of your investment and sets up a better expectations for you and your marketing dollars. As always, if it's measured, you'll know for sure how effective your spend per marketing channel was.

Finding a profitable marketing channel might be challenging at first, but it's not impossible. The key is to nail down your market and message first before even thinking about looking at the media on which you'll spend your money.

Before you get into media, though, explore the other strategies of inbound and social marketing before diving into this.

FAQ:

Don't we need an ad agency to do these things?

No. Ad agencies are struggling because the broad brushing they do with TV commercials, radio ads, and other traditional methods just isn't working anymore. Most people can fast forward through commercials now, anyway. You can hire someone internally or work with someone who works exclusively in the financial sector, but don't hire a PR or ad agency—they charge a lot for a little.

When do we see ROI from all this?

It depends. Inbound marketing can take months before you see returns. Outbound strategies can start right away. It's all about execution and following through. You can't afford to *not* spend the time marketing. Drop the non-billable admin tasks and start getting new clients!

Conclusion

This chapter is one of the longest in this book because I love to chat about marketing and I know that in CPA firms, marketing is often lacking. Partners are happy to spend their valuable time doing small compliance projects and admin tasks rather than bringing in millions of dollars in new clients.

Remember, bringing in more clients will bring in more income for you personally, as well as grow your firm and personal brand. As a partner, you are responsible for helping grow the firm. Doing $500 tax returns does not contribute to that goal.

You've also discovered the importance of your market and message and you've read about strategies, including inbound marketing, social media and networking.

Once you get these prospects interested, the time will come to close the sale. This is where you can start getting sweaty palms. Look, sales takes practice, practice and more practice. Successful partners put themselves out there knowing if they don't get this prospect, there will always be another. Have that abundance mindset. Plus, these sales tactics are so powerful, you can use them in everyday life.

Take this chapter and read it again and again. Give it to your team and other partners to read. After that, dive into the next section, and re-read that one again and again as well.

Action Steps

1. Revisit your market and message. Is it concrete and easy for clients and prospects to understand?

2. Determine the medium that would be best for your ideal clients. Have you created content for your client base?

3. Have a dedicated staff member to build your inbound strategies and create content. When should start this?

4. Check your LinkedIn profile and have each team member dedicate 30 minutes a day on LinkedIn to connect with your ideal client base.

5. Stop going to networking events that are sucking up time and not helping grow the firm. Could you be doing something wrong at these events?

Interviews to Go Deeper

1. Using Social Media and Other Strategies to Grow - with Jody Padar (https://jetpackworkflow.com/5-simple-steps-to-transform-into-a-radical-cpa-firm/)

2. How to Massively Profit on Your Expertise - with Seth David (https://jetpackworkflow.com/profit-on-your-expertise-seth-david/)

3. Getting Your Ideal Clients - with Nate Hagerty (https://jetpackworkflow.com/nate-hagerty-interview-get-ideal-accounting-clients/)

4. Using Content to Build Up a Client Base - with Edward Mendlowitz (https://jetpackworkflow.com/edward-

mendlowitz-interview-grow-accounting-firm-manage-staff/)

5. Free Marketing Strategies for Your Firm - with Bonnie Buol Ruszczyk (https://jetpackworkflow.com/free-marketing-strategies-for-your-firm-the-bonnie-buol-ruszczyk-interview/)

6. 47 Lead Generation Tips & Tricks (https://jetpackworkflow.com/47-lead-generations-tips-accountants/)

7. The New Rules of Marketing for CPA Firms (https://jetpackworkflow.com/new-rules-marketing-accounting-professionals/)

Recommendations

This chapter is the longest in the book because I've seen so many small to medium size firms drop the ball in this area. The landscape for marketing your firm has drastically changed since pre-2000, where you could bank on referrals and country club networking. That has changed and now your marketing strategy should as well.

None of this is easy to implement right away. That is why I want to offer you, as readers, two bonuses:

1. Up to one hour on the phone with me, *for free*, discussing your firm and the ideas and steps you need to get going. No obligation except that you have read this chapter.

2. A 10–20-page personalized report designed just for your firm, writing up these steps, that you can use as a reference going forward.

I can only do this a few times a quarter because of the time commitment, but this book is special to me. You deserve something special as well for being a reader.

To get started, email me at joe@jccopy.com with the subject line "Let's Rock This" I read every email.

Chapter 4

Your Sales Appointment Start to Close

Sales is likely a word that has a negative connotation to you, more than any other function of business. Because of this, most owners and partners shy away from ever investing in sales for the fear they'll transform into someone who is too "salesy," thereby bringing up past negative experiences.

If you're one of those owners who always views sales as a necessary evil, and you daydream of having clients just magically show up, then this chapter might not be for you. Sales is not something that is evil or negative. In fact, we strongly believe the opposite.

Great salespeople are value-driven, helpful advisors. The sign of a great salesperson is the ability to say, "We're not a good fit," because ultimately, if you serve someone who doesn't need your service, they're going to be a nightmare, take up a considerable amount of your time, and will eventually leave anyway.

Knowing and being comfortable with the fact that not *everyone* is your ideal customer should be a relief. Now, your job is to find the clients that are a perfect for the firm.

Simply put, great sales—and business—starts with solving a pain or need. The job of sales is to uncover the pain, understand the prospect's goals, and if you know you can help them achieve that goal, do everything in your power to assist them in becoming a client.

Can you imagine having a cure for lower back pain and keeping it to yourself because you were nervous about selling? What a loss for the world! It's the same with your service. If you can help individuals or businesses, then why not tell them?

The goal is to first *focus on the pain*, then connect to your solution. As a good friend of mine would say, "Follow the pain."

The practice of selling takes patience. Much like anything you do, at first, you will mess up. In the past, you've probably blown a sale in some fashion. We all have.

But when you have a roadmap to follow throughout the sale, you can follow it all the way to a successful close. It doesn't mean you will stay on the road at all times, but you will realize at which points you tend to veer away from the map and figure out ways to come back to it.

Now, there are entire sections in libraries about this one topic alone. So, as a disclaimer, don't be surprised if every little detail of selling isn't included. I recommend you read one of my favorite books, *You Can't Teach a Kid to Ride a Bike at a Seminar* by David Sandler. Much of my success and learning how to sell has come from that method and it's been tested over and over again.

In the sections below, we'll cover the outline for creating a sales script, common closes, how to create referrals from sales, and more.

The Mindset and Steps of a Successful Salesperson

"I'm not a salesperson."

The actual secret of the best salesmen in the world is that they behave more like advisors than salesmen. Much like you do when you're networking, they listen, ask questions, and then prescribe the solution.

Think of a doctor. If you walked into a doctor's office with a broken hand and he took one swift look at you up and down, then prescribed a cold medicine, you would be upset. You would think, *"The doctor didn't listen to me to find out what's wrong."*

As a CPA, you live in the analytical world. In sales, this can act as your superpower. Your perception of the needs of your prospect is an asset, when compared to the salesman who blabs the entire time about their service.

It's entirely possible for someone who has never made a sale to become great at capturing new clients, but it takes practice, determination, and patience.

Your first step is to change your mindset. Growing your firm should be a major motivation for you, whether you want to see more dividends, spend less time at the office, or take home more income. If you bring sales to a firm, your status catapults and you gain all of these benefits.

As a partner, it is your responsibility to grow your firm. Sitting behind your desk doing the same work as a first-year CPA stunts the growth of thousands of firms. By reading this section, you are taking the first step to buck this trend.

Steps to Selling

Before you jump on a call or agree to meet at a prospect's office, you need to consider the goals for the appointment. Think about what you want to do before jumping in, so you get what you need from the call. Here are the steps:

1. Qualify the prospect.
2. Pitch the service.
3. Find the problems.

4. Get them to the next step.

5. Build rapport.

Every prospect is different. If you already know their budget, you need to uncover their pain. But if it's just an initial meeting and you know nothing about them, you should want to build rapport.

At some point, you will do all five of these steps for a qualified prospect. With that in mind, you must also *feel out* why your prospect is meeting with you. What are their goals? Do they want to:

- kick the tires?
- shop price and compare you to competitors?
- educate themselves on whether or not they need your help?
- get free consulting?

You need to understand that prospects, no matter their background, feel okay with lying to someone who is selling to them. It goes back to the stigma of the untrustworthy salesperson. Thus, prospects feel better about leading you on or lying.

This is a main reason why you can feel good about building rapport with a prospect, but you can't get attached. You must be ready to pack it in if the deal isn't going to close.

Going into an appointment, you should know your goal, but also have the roadmap to get there. Here is a basic outline of a typical sales meeting:

1. **Constantly ask questions.**
   a. Ask about their struggles, their business, what's working, what's not, their family, their "why."

b. Dig in to find common ground on which to build rapport and trust.

c. Much like networking, asking questions keeps the prospect talking. The more they talk, the more they will give away. You must listen and not just think about the next question you want to ask.

2. **Search and search for pain points.**

a. When you hear something that could be a pain, simply say "Tell me more..."

b. Ask them "Why?" again and again.

c. Allow them to sit with their pain, don't acknowledge it, actually rub it in.

3. **Reveal the solution that is your solution.**

a. Take their pain and pair it with your offering.

b. Provide social proof of your results and discuss similar clients.

c. Reiterate how you're there as a trusted advisor and friend.

d. Ask them: *"Do you want to hear more?"* then wait for them to allow you to tell them.

4. **Knock out objections.**

a. You will hear many objections and you can address all of them. Your goal is to get them to a "yes," where you put together the proposal and next appointment time.

b. If you get stuck with so many objections and wishy-washy answers, you haven't fully addressed the pain points. Go back and try again.

5. **Keep the car moving forward.**

    a. Follow up with them, provide them value in some way so you stay top-of-mind.

    b. Understand that not everyone can become a client. Sometimes, it's a numbers game. A "no" is an opportunity to move forward. It means you can close out the account and move on to the next person without wasting time.

That's the basic roadmap for where you should be going at your sales meetings. Although that's the general structure, you still need to lead the prospect through this map without it coming across as fake or scripted. Let me take you through some strategies that work for my clients.

First Meeting with a Prospect

There's a great scene in the television comedy, *The Office*, where Michael Scott, regional manager of a paper company and known to say the wrong thing most of the time, with his boss, Jan, go to meet a prospect at a restaurant. Although Michael is notoriously clueless, he was also the top salesmen in the company.

As they sit down with the prospect, Jan, an inexperienced saleswoman, immediately wants to talk business with the prospect. The prospect is clearly tired and doesn't look interested. Michael, being great at sales, begins to talk over Jan, making wisecrack remarks and jokes. He even goes so far to sing songs and jingles with the prospect as they enjoy their food.

Jan starts getting annoyed, thinking Michael has proven to be the idiot once again and blown the sale. Then, just at the perfect time, Michael swoops in with his sales pitch and closes the client in under a minute. He had gotten the prospect so comfortable that the close was easy.

That's the power of rapport. Mind you, they already knew the prospect had a problem, they were just having trouble closing the deal. Rapport and making the prospect feel *at ease*, can go a long way. The small talk is important!

Build Rapport

Whether you enjoy small talk or not, it's essential to begin every meeting with trying to gain rapport in some way.

Whenever you meet a stranger on an airplane or at the park, normally there is some commonality you share with them. Perhaps you both have a dog or live in the same city. In a sales appointment, just like at a chance meeting, you must work to find some commonality.

You must make the prospect feel *at ease*. They need to feel comfortable with you in the situation, because they must willingly open themselves up to a sale. The best way to ensure that happens is to connect with them.

You can start with standard chatter topics, like:

- *"How are things in the X industry?"*
- *"Did you watch the game last night?"*
- *"How's the weather where you are?"*

All you want to do is make them feel at ease.

The best way to get there the fastest is to *let the prospect be smarter.* When you start using buzzwords or talking over their head, you aren't gaining respect, but you are losing the attention of your prospect. Ask the prospect obvious questions about their business, and make them feel important and intelligent. Ask questions you know the answer to, just to let them feel good about themselves.

David Cristello & Joe Cassandra

Once you hit a lull and the prospect feels a bit more comfortable, move to the next step.

Outline What Will Happen in The Meeting

After you build rapport, you need to *set the agenda*. As the saying goes, *"Most people have a secret desire to be led."* Setting an agenda allows the prospect to know what you will talk about.

You might say, *"Before we get too deep, can we set an agenda so this meeting is valuable to you and doesn't waste your time? Typically, I will ask you some questions about your business. We can chat about your last 12 months and how everything went. Dig into how the firm is doing as a whole. And then, if it makes sense, I can tell you about what I do. At that point, you can tell me if you want to move forward. Does that sound good for you?"*

A problem most amateur salesmen commit is letting the prospect control the conversation. If that happens, you're in a bad spot. Setting an agenda lets you control the chariot, even if the prospect comes out swinging asking, "Ok, what do you got? How much is it?" If that happens, all you do is slowly step back and redefine the objectives of the appointment.

When you take these steps, at the end of the meeting you will have a clear picture of where you stand. Basically, you are getting a "yes" up front to make a decision at the end about moving forward. You want a "yes" or a "no," and you definitely don't want a "maybe."

Only after getting the simple, "yes" to your agenda-setting question, should you move on to the next step.

Qualify the Prospect

After you've set the agenda, you will start digging into what they need. You do this by asking *why they wanted to talk with you.* Say, "Ok, we know what the goal is. Now, tell me what compelled you to want to talk with me?"

Don't let a prospect off the hook. They may give you a quick, "I wanted to see if you can help me." So dig more. Say, "Tell me about that, who was your previous firm? Why weren't they a good fit?" Keep going with follow-up questions and don't acknowledge their problems, just keep digging for them until you find the gold.

You want to find out their deep motivations for talking to you. Did their last firm drop the ball? Is the prospect simply price shopping? Have they just recently grown and need a firm for the first time?

If they've never had an accounting firm before, you can ask, *"What's causing you to stop doing it internally? What happened in the last 12 months?"*

These questions have one goal: qualify your prospect to see if it's worth the time to continue the conversation. You're listening for little pieces of information that signal to you they could make sense as a client and fit under your ideal prospect.

Once you get the client talking, start to probe further.

Find their Pain Points

While you dig, move into them *talking out and recognizing their pain.*

At this stage, you are only *asking* questions and making them vocalize the problems they face. Perhaps you find out from the previous questions that they are leaving their old CPA firm because of cash flow problems. The business owner feels cash is always tight.

At this point, many do the wrong thing. They start talking about solutions to overcome the cash flow issue.

WRONG!

You aren't giving solutions yet. You need to probe further down this rabbit hole. The more pain a prospect feels, the more likely they will be open to your solutions. Remember, you are in control of the sale. While the prospect is talking about cash flow problems, the deeper pain might be that they can't provide for their newborn daughter or their spouse just lost his/her job.

These are the real pain points and you need to drag them out them so they say it out loud and realize the trouble they are in. Again, you are not solving the problems here. The prospect may even ask about you helping with their issue.

The wrong answer is, *"Of course! Let me tell you about it!"*

The right answer would be, *"I'm not sure yet, let's talk more. Tell me more about why it's so important to you on a business and personal level."*

Every sale you make, whether you sell something exotic like a seven-day cruise to South America, or hammers and nails, is emotionally charged. People buy based on *how they feel* and then rationalize it with logic. The more pain you dig into, the more emotional the prospect gets.

You can do this by not letting them think you feel for them. Don't say, "I bet that's hard," or "Oh yes, many clients have that problem." You want them to feel somewhat bad about their situation so they are compelled to change.

A person is compelled to change when he/she feels they are on the outside or different from others. If every business owner has the problem, they don't feel as bad and thus aren't as interested in changing.

This step is powerful, but fragile. The key is for the prospect to realize they need the pain to go away *right now*. At the same time, you don't want to tell them what they should do. That would be embarrassing.

As an example, you want your prospect to verbalize why fixing their cash flow is important to them on both a business and personal level. Let them tell you about supporting their daughter or helping their spouse during the job search. They must tell you about needing to solve this pain to help them, not you.

Don't say, "You know, if you don't fix this cash flow problem, you'll have many problems supporting your daughter. You won't be able to support your spouse as they look for a job and that could hurt your marriage…"

You are addressing the pain, which is good, but this isn't the right approach. All it does is embarrass a prospect. You want them to discover for themselves how important it is to fix the problem.

The list of pain questions you can ask is limitless, but they should all focus around a problem. Consider these:

- How are you currently solving this problem you mentioned?
- Are you comfortable running your business with this problem?
- Do you believe this is a severe problem?
- Is there anything about your situation you don't like?
- How long has this been a problem?

- Do you have any problems related to [BLANK]? You could lead them towards the problems you solve.
- It sounds like you are unhappy with your [BLANK], right?

Make them sit with their pain. They will feel vulnerable and a tad uncomfortable, but they are not uncomfortable with you. It's their situation that makes them uncomfortable. The point isn't to make them feel bad, but to bring to light their problems so they understand how important it is to resolve those issues.

Normally, you will need to dig further down as many of the first answers they give won't be the real pain. Make sure, with each point they mention, you ask at least two follow ups:

- "Tell me more about that…"
- "Can you give me an example?"
- "How do you really feel about this?"

Once you get them to express their pain, let them open up more.

Find Out What Their Goal Is

As they feel vulnerable, now you need them to vocalize what they want. Ask them:

- What would you like to see different in your business?
- How would your personal life change?
- How would things be different in your business if you fixed this?
- What's your goal for growing this business in terms of revenue?

Here, you want them to get excited for the future. Push them to dream big and visualize how their business will be so much better if they had a solution to their pain.

Then, expose why they can't do this themselves. Make them admit it. How? Just ask!

> *"Ok, you want to get to [X goal]. What's stopping you from doing this yourself?"*

If they have the pain and could solve it themselves, you probably wouldn't be talking to them. If they can solve it themselves, you probably won't close them as a client and should just politely end the call.

It's the perfect moment as they already feel comfortable being open with you and you can ask about budget.

Ask How Much They Will Pay

Asking about money may be the hardest thing. The topic lingers over your head, but it needs to be touched on. Of course, no one wants to bring it up first. This step can also be done at the very beginning. Because, well, why dig for pain and go through that whole process only to realize the prospect has no money to pay you?

To do that, simply come from a vulnerable position as you set the stage of the meeting:

> *"John, I'll be honest with you. The hardest part of these initial meetings for me is discussing the money portion. It makes me uncomfortable. Is it OK if we get money out of the way early?* [Prospect says "Sure."] *Great, thank you so much. So, quickly, what price range would you feel comfortable with to help with your financial and accounting needs?"*

Then, be quiet. Let them ponder for a second and give you a range. If it's far lower than what you charge, it might be easiest to simply say, *"Hmm, I would take you as someone who would invest more into this. If you can't invest more than that, I'm not sure if there's anything I could do to help. Should we close this out before we dive in further?"*

If they say, "No." You can follow up with, *"Well, what if the solution requires an investment higher than what you planned?"*

You want to get a range to see if they have the money, but also to see how much they value your services. You could be leaving thousands of dollars on the table each month because you don't see how valuable your clients consider your services.

Have you heard about billionaires paying tens of millions of dollars for paintings? What's funny is a handful of these paintings look very simple, yet through the lens of the billionaire, it's worth the price. You must believe what you offer is valuable, so the client feels they will get an ROI just by using you rather than a cheaper option.

Never assume something is too expensive until a client tells you it is. You never know your prospect's budget, so it's your responsibility to get them to tell you. If they aren't being honest with you or they dance around the subject, they most likely don't have a budget at all and they are price shopping. This is a red flag.

If the prospect says, "I don't have a budget." They may not have a specific dollar figure, but you can coax it out of them by offering a range. Say, "John, we discussed Problem 1, 2 and 3. I might have a solution for you. Let's first clarify where you are, since you don't know your budget. Our solutions range from $2,000–$5,000 and from $6,000–$20,000. Which range would you want to address first?"

Most likely, they will mention bracket that feels more comfortable. Now, you can go forward.

As a quick note, this step reveals the prospect's budget, *not* what you charge for your work. You can give them a range, but don't get into specific pricing until you extract the pain, or none of this will work.

Get Them to Commit

After getting them to admit they need the help and telling you their budget, move into gaining commitment. You want them to verbalize that they need help soon.

You ask, *"When do you want to fix this? I know you want to fix it, but I'm wondering how committed you are to doing it now...?"*

Remember, in the beginning, you want to set the agenda that the appointment will end in clear next steps. Either, "Yes, let's keep going," or "No, we are done."

Another great question to get them interested in you presenting your solution is, *"You've gotten to where you are, why not just stay there?"*

If they are still hanging with you and answering your questions, ask permission to tell them your solution.

Offer Your Solution

Give them the illusion of control and ask for permission to tell you about your firm. Say, *"It sounds like I can help you. Would you like me to tell you about what I do?"*

State your services and how they tie into the prospect's various pain points. You want to get them to the proposal stage and schedule a time for the follow up.

Explain your firm's "why" and how it helps them. You don't want to just agree to a proposal. Proposals get stuck on desks and are forgotten.

You need to schedule a time to go through the proposal with them, no ifs, ands, or buts.

Clarification About Proposals and Pricing

In Chapter 2, we discussed preparing proposals with various options. You definitely want to present this to the prospect. In the beginning, it might be best to agree to a proposal and find a time to talk it over.

As you do more and more of this, you will be able to pull together options on the fly based on your products and get a pricing structure right away. This will be powerful because your prospect will be primed and ready for you to solve their pain *right now*. It's best to be ready to offer your bundle of services and get them to a "yes" or a "no."

Many business owners go through a process before jumping into a new firm. In that case, hold off giving pricing and make sure you prepare the best proposal and get them on the phone to discuss it. The more touch points you have, the better.

> **Quick tip:** *To speed up the sales process, I've used an "incentive-based pricing" approach. Essentially, if they sign the deal within X amount of days, they get a discount of some sort as a reward for making the decision to move forward. Bringing that up during the pricing stage is best because it adds urgency to the moment.*

Overcoming Objections

Look back over the follow-up section in Chapter 3 for responding to wishy-washy answers. At the end of this appointment, you want a clear path to a "yes" or a "no." If they are hesitating, challenge them on that and turn it around.

A major hurdle you will face is you prospect telling you, *"I need to think it over."* You need a strategy to get around this, so let me tell you what I've done in the past.

When meeting with a prospect about my services, things were going well, but when I got to the end of the sales call, he gave me the *"I will think it over."* A line you will hear again and again.

Most amateurs would say *"Of course, whatever you need."* And they will never hear from the prospect again. Instead, I challenged him. I said, *"John, I understand you need to think about. What do you need to think about?"*

He told me he needed to weigh the options against my competitors, so I said, *"Ok, that makes sense, I would do the same thing. Let me ask you this, what would you have to see on my end to make you comfortable with moving forward?"*

We worked it out and now we're working together each month. The point is to always be direct, but not pushy with a prospect. Remember, they are comfortable lying to you.

Sales trainer and consultant, Martin Bissett, stopped by and offered solutions to the common four objections he hears regularly. Here's how you can overcome them:

1. **"I will think about it…"** — Martin recommends, as I do, to simply get a date on the calendar to talk it over. If they aren't willing to set a time, they aren't interested.

2. **"We are going on vacation next week…"** (or any other unrelated issue) — This is a classic stall tactic. To get around it, your job will be to convince them to get locked-in today. Use incentive-based pricing or another similar tactic. *"Your vacation doesn't affect this problem…let's discuss this…"*

3. **"Why should I pay more for your service?"** *(and any other half-truths)* — You might believe this is a price war question but actually, the prospect can't see the added value

you bring. Your response centers around the massive value your firm brings to the table.

4. *"We are bankrupt...have health problems...are in a legal battle right now..."* — Answer? Nothing. You can't reverse this and it's a red flag that this prospect might have trouble paying you.

Martin reminds us that your client's objections are not *personal attacks.* They are the knee-jerk reactions people have when they don't want to make a decision. Objections can even come in the form of lies.

I've had prospects tell me: *"Send me over the agreement to get started,"* and I never hear from them again. The sale isn't closed until the agreement is signed and the check is written!

Don't ever assume. That's one major don't, but here are some *do's.*

Quick Tips for Better Selling

1. **The power of silence:** When you ask a question, don't embellish. Ask the question, then sit in silence. Even if it's an uncomfortable silence. The line, "Whoever speaks first, loses" is true in sales. Silence is powerful.

2. **Reverse every objection:** Never accept an objection. Always reverse it. I've sprinkled examples throughout this chapter. "What specifically do you need to talk about, can I clear it up now?" "When do you plan to speak with them?"

3. **Be willing to let them go:** "To be honest, John, you don't seem that interested at the moment, and that's OK. It would save us both time if we close this out right now. Do you agree?" If they do, they will say yes. If they were hoping to string you along to get a better price, they will beg for you not to leave.

Conclusion

You have the roadmap here, but it would be helpful, as I've found, to write out the process yourself. It sticks in your head more and you can organize how you want your sales appointment to go.

You're more than likely going to need to practice this multiple times. You'll mess up and lose some sales. Just like learning to ride a bike, brush your knees off and start again. This is a proven map to a successful sale in business and your daily life.

Learning to sell is one of the mai skills your firm needs. Your business will go bankrupt without a solid sales process and a dedicated person to close deals.

Action Steps

1. Write out this process by hand in a format you find easiest to follow. Read through it multiple times each week, especially as you get closer to an upcoming sales appointment.

2. Listen for objections in your daily life. Find ways to reverse them and get the sale moving again. Perhaps you're trying to convince your child or spouse of something; try a handful of these tactics to practice. They can work everywhere!

Resources

1. *You Can't Teach a Kid to Ride a Bike at a Seminar* by David Sandler, Sandler Sales Training

2. How to Handle Objections and Close the Sale - with Martin Bissett (https://jetpackworkflow.com/top-sales-objection-close-clients/)

Recommendations

Going into a sales appointment gets easier and easier the more you do it. On top of that, when you market your firm correctly, prospects come in pre-sold.

To start the brainstorming process to make your sales appointments run smoother, you might want to take advantage of this free offer.

1. Up to one hour on the phone with me, *for free*, discussing your firm and the ideas and steps you need to get going. No obligation except that you have read this chapter.

2. A 10–20-page personalized report designed just for your firm, writing up these steps, that you can use as a reference going forward.

I can only do this a few times a quarter, because of the time commitment, but this book is special to me. You deserve something special as well for being a reader.

To get started, email me at joe@jccopy.com with the subject line "Let's Rock This." I read every email.

Chapter 5

Get Referrals and Attract the Clients You Want

Darren Root, Founder of Rootworx and renowned influencer and speaker in the accounting world, built a firm into seven figures before the age of 30. But he was unhappy. He spent so much time in the office and almost no time at home with his wife and three kids. Something had to change.

One morning, he woke up as normal and fired 80% of his clients and sent them to a competitor. He kept the remaining 20% and used them build his company. That small group represented his favorite clients, who he actually enjoyed working with.

To have a firm grow and do so well while still enjoying your life and work is the definition of success. For many firms, success rests solely on a dollar figure per year. What if you could reach that same figure but only with clients you actually enjoy working with?

You could stop just accepting *everyone who has a wallet*. Many might not be the right fit for you, yet you continue to work with them. Even millionaires stress about their money because they worry it could all be gone, so we put up with clients we don't enjoy just to pad the accounts a bit.

In Chapter 3, we went through how to market your firm and bring in clients like clockwork, using inbound strategies, LinkedIn and networking. A last piece to the pie is referrals.

It makes my head spin when firm owners brag about *"not having to spend any money on marketing,"* because of the referrals they get. Referrals are unpredictable. Yes, they are nice, but doubling your firm requires systems and predictability. Referrals and marketing must have a system.

Referrals can bring in your best clients. It's proven. Referrals pay more, on average, than clients brought in other ways. It's a catch-22 as referrals are often unpredictable, as well. This is why I recommend the two-pronged approach of marketing and referrals.

If you are bringing in new clients every week who you love working with, you're in a great spot. I would still absolutely recommend working through the marketing strategies in Chapter 3 as a two-pronged attack to growth.

You might already see a trickle of referrals coming in organically. We can jumpstart that even more. Jay Abraham considers waiting for referrals to be *passive*, but getting them to come on their own is *active*.

Being passive with referrals is the reason firms don't see more referrals or get the type of referrals they want. They are afraid of making their clients uncomfortable, but you can bring in active referrals without it being uncomfortable or feeling salesy.

Before you even think about going after referrals though, you must start with your confidence. Successful referrals begin with 100% confidence and love for what you offer. If you don't have this confidence and love, it comes across to your clients.

Think about one team member who absolutely can't live without doing accounting work and argues its importance as compared with someone who is unsure about each tax return that goes out the door and isn't enthusiastic with clients. I guarantee the former will get more referrals than the latter.

In this chapter, you'll flesh out *why* your clients pick you, especially your best ones. This makes it easier to ask for referrals later on. We will also touch on points from Chapter 1 to help you bring on clients that are the right fit for the firm. Then, we'll go through how to nurture your clients to make them *want* to refer you. Finally, I will tell you the absolute best methods for asking for referrals.

But first, let's start off with a review of terms.

Your Unique Selling Point

We've gone over your USP already, so if you don't remember this, you will want to go back and review prior chapters. When you've done that, come back with your USP.

Before we get into this section, you should know the value you want to bring to the marketplace and what type of clients you wish to attract. Remember, you must have a target market and message.

Your market is the type of industry and/or service you wish to be an expert in. For example, you might want to be the go-to CPA firm for construction companies.

Then, your message attracts your market as you highlight the results you bring to your ideal client base. Earlier, we used this example: *we help seven- and eight-figure construction companies automate their back office finances, so they can they increase cash flow, grow faster, and save more money on their returns.*

These form the basis for your USP. Your next step is figuring out how your clients view your USP. What do you solve for them?

The easiest way to do this is to just ask! Sit down individually with a handful of clients you trust and enjoy working with. You can do that by sending them this email:

"Hi [Client Name],

Looking forward to discussing how last quarter went. At the end of our meeting, would you be able to take an extra 10 minutes to give me feedback on how our relationship is going and addressing your good and bad experiences?

Thanks,

Joe

Most clients would be happy to do this. Your goal is to figure out what you do better than others that your clients recognize. Questions you can ask, include:

- What keeps you coming back to work with us each year?
- What do you enjoy most about working with us?
- What trouble spots have you found?
- How does our relationship compare to other firms you've worked with in the past?

All you're looking for is a pattern for what you do better.

- *"You always sound happy to answer all my questions."*
- *"You've saved me more money than any other firm."*
- *"I get my work on time."*
- *"You always exceed my expectations for each engagement."*

These are just examples. The reason this is critical is because your ideal clients will be similar in many ways to your current, most trusted clients. Your ideal clients might all value punctuality, great service, and consistency.

These traits allow you to form an avatar of who you wish to work with. We already discussed, in Chapter 3, how to narrow down your market and client avatar. This USP allows you to speak to and nurture your current client base to prime them to refer others to you.

As you talk with new prospects, you will be able to compare notes to what your ideal client wants and what a new prospect might look for. "Birds of a feather…" comes into play here.

Obviously, before working with a client, you won't know how they act and work. These clues towards your USP or away from it can provide that much-needed insight.

Your first steps are to set up a time with 3–5 of your best clients and ask them these questions. In your day-to-day interactions, take note of when they compliment your work or thank you. Those can clue you into what they believe your USP is.

Bringing on the Right Clients

As another review from prior chapters, your client base can make or break your team. A major issue in firms, at the moment, is retaining the best and brightest talent, especially for the future.

With referrals, clients will tend to refer other clients like them. If your bad clients are referring more bad clients, you run into a disastrous problem. Your top clients may not know the steps to referring correctly, so you might not get referrals from them.

The fewer conversations you can have with referrals from your bad clients, the better, I'm certain. For example, you might decide your core market is medical professionals, but your lone car dealership client keeps referring in other dealerships and it overwhelms your team. At the same time, if your car dealership client isn't a great client, most likely his referrals will be of the same caliber.

That could be a demoralization bomb.

This all rolls back to your sales process and onboarding, coupled with your USP. Ask yourself during the initial stages, these questions:

- Is this client right for the firm?
- Do they appear similar to my ideal clients?
- What do they believe our USP is?
- Do they respect me?

You will get referrals from outside your ideal market and they could be fantastic clients. You still need to run them through your USP tests to find the similarities they share with your ideal prospects.

During the initial discussions, you are listening to their pain. Bring up your USP and see how it works with the new client. Is your USP resonating with them or are they solely focused on another point?

These are the red flags to watch out for before signing on the bottom line.

Go back to Chapter 1 to learn more about onboarding correctly and making sure they are the right fit. These are the pillars for setting your clients up for sending over referrals.

What you can expect is, for anyone, pushing their friends into a sales pitch isn't what they typically wish to do. It's the reason you need to make sure you are nurturing and caring for your clients as you go, to make them feel comfortable to send their friends and colleagues to you.

Nurturing Your Current Clients

"Become a trusted advisor, not just a paper-cruncher."

Shelley Johnson, Managing Partner of Allman Johnson CPAs, has grown her firm organically through the years.

Clients continue to come back to her firm because a deeper relationship forms when the client–CPA relationship gets tossed out and a more personal relationship takes its place. Too often you will get bogged down in the weeds with deadline stress and various projects that come up.

What happens, then, is you only talk to a client in January and swap emails and calls until April 15th. Compare that to how Shelley will advise you to approach it. She asks herself, *"Which client can I help today and who may need it?"*

For bonus points, her firm works on a fixed pricing model, so clients can feel comfortable on the phone without worrying about a bombshell on their bill.

As you develop your market and your message, you will be more honed in on your ideal client's industry. This allows you to relate to them more personally with advice based on the industry and understand their situation much better.

Your first step to nurturing current clients is asking, *"Where can I provide even more value?"*

Steve Pipe, founder of ImproveYourPractice, has five checklist items to make sure clients are getting enough value and the right kind of it. His five points are:

1. Do something *before* a client requests it. Read their mind and know their needs.

2. Make a special deliverable absolutely relevant to them, perhaps a piece of content based on a recent discussion. This does not apply to your monthly newsletter.

3. Provide something that makes a difference in their personal or work life.

4. Do something special for them and do it pro bono the first time as a surprise for them.

5. Duplicate it across clients. Systematize the benefit.

Nurturing a client goes far beyond just doing your work. Where can you "wow" a client so they always remember and think of you?

Every interaction with a client is an opportunity to nurture them. Perhaps they are having a rough day and need someone to listen. Instead of ushering them off the phone, take the extra 15 minutes and listen to what they have to say. When your client tells you they are distracted because their air conditioner just went out, send them a referral to your local A/C man.

The more a client trusts you, the more they open up to you. When you know them better, you can solve more of their problems, meaning you can come up with more service offerings. Clients will pay for you to solve their problems, so the more valuable you come across to them, the more they are likely to pay for your services and keep coming back to you.

Steve says, "Stand up for premium services. Higher prices attract better clients." You can charge more when you constantly go above and beyond because you aren't a commodity anymore.

Let's look at the stages of a new client into a great client.

Know → *Like* → *Trust*

A client comes to know about you, so this is the easiest step. After which, they like you enough to do business with you. For many, that's where it stops, but trust is the staple for a successful client who will then refer you more clients like them.

To build that trust, you must ask these questions:

- Am I up to date with all the industry trends?
- Do I have testimonials from happy clients on my website?
- Are there rewards I've won which should be displayed?
- Do I create content that helps a client when the time comes?
- Do I offer consults my clients gladly pay for?

We mentioned, in Chapter 3, how critical content can be to your firm. By reading this book, you're already coming out ahead of most firms who believe *just the work* is what clients want.

We are in the information age. Experts who can provide us the right information at the right time become valuable to our networks. The Internet has helped create this demand. It has also made adding value for your clients much easier.

Sales Trainer David Fisher makes a point to schedule *at minimum*, a 15-minute personal call with clients every six months in which you talk about how their business is changing, their personal lives, and more. It works for new connections as well. Take an invested interest outside of the workplace with your clients.

Are there ways to add value outside of the scope of your projects? Of course, there are plenty. Consider these options:

- **Invite them out to dinner:** Surprise a client with an invitation for dinner with your significant other and theirs, if applicable. Bringing your spouse allows the conversation to expand past work and gets both you and your client to open up more with each other. Expect major rapport building.

- **Send them a webinar invite:** Webinars are all the rage in today's information age. If you just had a conversation with a client about slumping sales, send them a link to a webinar you just found about finding new clients. Drop them a note: *"We talked about this last week. I stumbled on this and it could give you some ideas on increasing customer acquisition. If it's something you think is helpful, let me know and I'll keep my eyes out for more."* Information is a powerful trust builder.

- **Bring them along to a conference:** If there's a conference a client might appreciate, drop them a note with an invitation.

- **Plan a fun event:** The old-school method of bringing your client out to a ball game is still relevant today. Try to keep business talk on a leash until later in the night so the client can relax first.

- **Ask their opinion:** Everyone loves to give their opinion and are flattered when asked for it. Ask your client for their opinion on a matter and listen.

- **Follow and interact with them on social media:** LinkedIn remains a powerful tool for keeping track of your clients outside of work. If you see a work anniversary or a new post from a client, give it as much love as you can without being creepy.

A special trust building tool I've used and done with the best intentions is to send gifts. Perhaps a book or something you run across they might appreciate. I've even sent personalized items for the client and their spouse as a token of goodwill, thanks, and utility.

A great tip for gifts: Avoid sending them during the holidays. Your clients are already bombarded with chocolate arrangements and flowers around that time. When you send it during the summer, they don't expect it and it will land the most impact.

Author and speaker Michelle Long, founder of Long for Success LLC, recommends, as we discussed in Chapter 3, to build out your circle of influence. Remember, your circle consists of professions outside of your own industry that interact regularly with your profession. For CPAs, this could be lawyers, insurance salesmen, financial software developers, or other related fields.

Michelle says to find complementary services you can continually send clients to. Much like we mentioned above, if your client is frustrated with a busted air conditioner, you can refer out. In Michelle's case, you want to refer to people who can refer back, like lawyers and financial planners.

Referring out to a complementary service builds massive trust. Renowned marketer Jay Abraham even shows examples of referring out to competitors. One accountant didn't do certain audit work, so he referred out the work to another CPA firm.

Clients trust you when you are willing to lose out on business to help them. If you've seen *Miracle on 34th Street*, you'll remember Kris Kringle sending parents to other toy stores than the one he worked in because it would be a better deal in another store. Soon, hundreds of parents and children were lining up to talk to Kris because of the trust he had sowed and the knowledge he bestowed.

You can do the same thing. Even better, I'll show you a way to do this and still make money, but that's later in the chapter.

Most clients will need to be in a certain state before they will give out referrals. This state is typically one where they fully trust everything you do and can't wait to tell others about you. Have you ever tried a new boutique restaurant and it was incredible? The first thing you want to do is tell others about it, partly because you found it before everyone else.

Clients have this same condition. They found you, they see the incredible value you provide and that you're always there for them, so they *must* tell others who haven't found you yet. It gives them satisfaction.

This is what you need to understand about client referrals. They don't do it to help you! For the most part, they honestly don't care if your business grows at all this year. They refer because it makes themselves feel good and helps their closest friends and neighbors.

Nurturing them correctly makes them want to tell others how great you are and makes them willing to go out of their way to do it.

All that's left now is to figure out how to ask your clients for those referrals. Let's do that now.

Asking for Referrals

It's great to read all of this, but the moment of truth comes when you're face-to-face with a client. Your mouth is dry and out comes, *"Umm, know anyone?"*

You client is bound to day, *"Nope."* And you'll likely respond, *"Oh, okay..."* [I will never ask this client again...]

Let me be frank, we build up in our head that a client is going to chew us out for asking for a referral. If it's a client you know well, you know you've built trust and added value, so the worst thing they will probably say is, *"I'll keep you in mind."*

That's it. Truth is, if you've done a great job for a client and you've worked with them for at least six months, popping the referral question isn't unprecedented.

It's because of this somewhat quick, but often awkward conversation, that partners will lean on passive referrals, instead. Those are always a fun surprise.

Business, however, grows on predictability. Becoming more active in the referral process welcomes that predictability. There's no need to be bashful. Your clients understand referrals are important to business and they probably bank on them as well.

But for a referral request to work, you must be in love with your product and service, and have the confidence that it is better than others'. Your client will hear your confidence when you recommend your services to their friends. No one wants to refer to someone who is unsure of themselves.

You have clients who love your work and stand by you. That's proof enough to give you confidence in what you do. This first step is crucial.

After getting your mindset right, you must set up the meeting. When you were building your USP, I gave you a script you can use for your clients to get that initial meeting. Here it is again for reference:

"Hi [Client Name],

Looking forward to discussing how last quarter went. At the end of our meeting, would you be able to take an extra 10 minutes to give me feedback on how our relationship is going and addressing your good and bad experiences?

Thanks,

Joe

It's after getting information like this, that you can get the client into a state where they trust you and are excited to tell others about you. Next, you want to massage their ego a bit and let them know how much your relationship means. Try something like this:

"John, I really enjoy working together with you. You're one of my favorite clients to help and it sounds like you are happy with everything we've done together so far, is that right?"

You want to make sure the client is listening, agrees with what you're saying, and gives you leeway to continue talking. Your client may even go off on a soliloquy about how much they love you! That works too.

Dan Allison, President of Broker's Clearing House and successful speaker on mastering referrals, recommends asking your client *how* they would like to be approached about referrals. He believes you should open yourself up to your client and show some vulnerability.

His script leans on this and indirectly asks for a referral through this process:

> *"I wanted to get your feedback on something. Our firm really likes to grow through helping our clients and people who are important to them. This can involve our clients referring us or introducing us to people that they know.*
>
> *As you know, this can be an uncomfortable topic. On one hand, every time I see my clients I could say, "Who do you know?" but I avoid doing this because I never want anyone to feel uncomfortable.*
>
> *On the other hand, if I avoid the topic altogether I may have an entire client base that doesn't even know whether or not we want to help more people.*
>
> *How can I approach the topic of referrals with you, if at all, in a way that will be comfortable for you and will not compromise the relationship that we have?"*

See the strategy? You are bringing up the elephant in the room, as asking for referrals is a tricky and somewhat uncomfortable business. Dan pushes through that barrier by bringing it up and listening to what the client says.

Dan's research points out that most clients don't refer automatically because the firm doesn't ask. Clients are waiting to be courted a bit before opening their contact list. Furthermore, they don't know how busy you are and might not want to add to your workload. Remove all these barriers from your client's mind and ensure you're on the same page. It could save you from an awkward conversation if a client prefers you don't ask for referrals.

After getting an affirmative answer from your client, you might be able to plunge right into asking for a referral or you might need to wait for the next time you chat. In any sense, you know how your client prefers to be asked and you can approach them with the right strategy.

For the actual asking portion, you should know the specifics about how you want to ask. There are a variety of methods you can use to get a referral out of a client.

Non-Client

A non-client referral might not be as powerful, as they haven't been in the trenches with you on a project like a client has, but there are many movers and shakers out in the world who could definitely bring clients to your door. Consider approaching people like,

Find a sample script you can use to send to your prospect in the Resources section of this chapter.

New Client—Aggressive

When the client is about to sign on the line, if you are confident about the progress you've made and you know you don't have to rely on this referral, consider this aggressive approach. Tell the client that working with you is a privilege and working with you requires referrals as part of admission.

Find a sample script in the Resources section of this chapter.

If that's a bit too much for your preference, let's scale it back a bit.

New Client—Discount

This is one of the more popular approaches. For new clients, it's not uncommon to offer some sort of commission for an introduction.

For example, I've bargained with clients to write a set of emails for free in exchange for three qualified referrals. For those emails, I would normally charge less than $2,000 and three new clients could be a five-figure windfall.

You can approach the client the same way as the aggressive approach.

You can find a sample script for this approach in the Resources section of this chapter.

Client—Approach #1

Diving into the legacy client side, here's an old trick I've heard from the greats. It's called the three business card approach.

How it works is you give your client three business cards, instead of the standard one and ask them to pass two of them along to anyone else who might be interested.

Find a sample script of this approach in the Resources section of this chapter.

Client—Approach #2

This is the best approach to use when you know your clients well, and you see what's coming along the pipeline for them. By listening to them, you can anticipate what they might need.

In this approach, you offer a free service to an existing client in exchange for referrals. For example, you could train your client's team on a new system in exchange for three quality referrals.

Using this method, you are offering a great service as an exchange—in many cases, your client might still pay you for your work!

Find an example script in the Resources section of this chapter.

Competitor Referral Trick

I mentioned earlier that if you send prospects who aren't a good fit for you to one of your competitors, you build massive trust with that competitor. It sounds counter-intuitive, but there is a way for it to be a win-win.

Work *with* your competitors to develop deals for sending over new work. Every small introduction can be quick profit.

There are points you can negotiate with them up front. For many partners, they get in an awkward position when they refer over to another professional and hope the recipient will send referrals back. Unfortunately, it doesn't always work this way. The recipient may not have any referrals for you, or they might perform similar services as you do and not want to pass over clients.

Rather than relying on hope for reciprocation, open the discussion yourself beforehand so as to avoid the uncomfortable positions of asking *"I send you referrals. Why don't you ever send me any?"*

This can be a difficult one to figure out, but with the script you'll find in the Resources section of this chapter, you'll create excellent relationships.

Email Signature

Your clients regularly see your email signature, whether consciously or subconsciously, and so providing a subtle reminder to them is a painless way to get the idea out there.

Here is an example of what you might write:

Our firm is built upon referrals and working with people just like you. We appreciate every referral we get. If you know someone who

*needs help with their business financials, we offer free consults for
new clients.*

It costs nothing, and there is no pressure on the client to do anything
if they don't think they should. At the same time, it makes your client
aware that referring their colleague or friend will be welcome.

Conclusion

The key to getting the right referrals starts with your USP. You must
know what your clients value before you can know exactly who the
right type of referrals are for your firm.

Remember, you don't want to attract everyone. Every referral is not
a great referral simply because the referral brings money to the table.
You are trying to build the *right* firm with the *right* clients. If the
referral doesn't fall into the "right clients" corner, take a pass.

As Darren Root says:

*"Let's create a company that does not depend on you, in which you
can create a product and be really good at delivering it, and then
find people to whom you want to deliver."*

Nurturing your clients sets the stage for asking for referrals. It requires
adding even more value, so find areas where you can go above and
beyond to solidify trust with your client.

Create content to give to your client at the right time, send personalized
gifts without a heads up or a holiday, and go from being a "paper-
cruncher" to a trusted advisor.

Lastly, all of this sounds great, but if you don't go for asking for the
referral, it won't mean much. You can go the aggressive approach of
demanding referrals from clients or the more conservative approach
of bargaining for referrals with discounts, bonus cash, or free work.

Find where you are most comfortable. Test out different blends of asking for referrals and see what is the most profitable and comfortable for you and your team. You'll find scripts to help you with each of these scenarios in the Resources section below.

Coupling marketing with knowing how to ask for referrals will provide you all the ammunition you need to blow up any worries about not having enough clients ever again.

Resources

Scripts for Asking for Referrals

Non-Client

Hi John,

I'm building out my company and thought of you. I've watched your path through X Company, and congrats on the recent promotion. Our chat a few months ago really stuck with me and I've taken your advice to your heart as I get this off the ground.

Your thoughts would be great: I'm focusing on helping financial companies get more clients through their marketing and sales copy. Are there any specific companies or individuals you recommend I reach out to?

Hope you and the wife are doing great, congrats on the pregnancy!

Joe

Notice I started with a bit of personalized catching up and letting John know how much I admire and respect him. Then, I moved into asking for his recommendation for companies and individuals. I don't say, *"Do you have a referral for me?"*

That doesn't give John the opportunity to say "No" without feeling uncomfortable. How I've phrased it, the worst thing John could say is, *"Nothing comes to mind."* See how much easier this makes it for him?

Also, notice I don't start with, "Hope you are well." It's a throwaway line. Instead, I actually compliment him. Putting, "Hope you are well!" at the end gives it much more meaning. Having it at the beginning puts John on alert, wondering, "What does he want...?"

New Client—Aggressive

"John, I pride myself in the work I do for my clients. Most of my new business comes from referrals, as you've seen. My clients refer me to others as a special thanks for the results I've brought them. A condition of doing business with me is you must provide me with three referrals at the point you are satisfied with the work I'm doing for you. Will this be a problem for you?"

This takes some guts to pull off. If you're in a position where clients are coming in swarms to work with you, this might be the best approach. If you've gone through the right vetting process and you feel this client will be the right fit, go for it.

New Client—Discount

"John, I pride myself in the work I do for my clients. Most of my new business comes from referrals, as you've seen. My clients refer me to others as a special thanks for the results I've brought them.

We've agreed on X deliverables at the price of $X per month. We can continue with this as agreed and have an awesome relationship. However, I like to incentivize clients to refer me to other professionals who might need similar help. I understand having you get referrals for me can be uncomfortable so I want to make sure to make it as comfortable as possible. If you are able to refer me three qualified *people, I'm more than happy to chop $X right up front. What do you think?"*

Here it is more conservative exchange.

You can also test the reverse and simply say, *"I give my clients $2,000 for each of their referrals who become clients."*

Some clients may see the bonus money as more valuable than a discount on a bill. Try both ways on new clients and see which sticks and which also brings in the most qualified clients.

Client—Approach #1

"John, you're one of my best clients and I know you have contacts that are great to work with as well. Here are three of my cards. You keep one, and if you come across an acquaintance or someone who needs similar tax and QuickBooks help like I've given you, please give them my card and have them call me for a free consult right up front. You were happy with my service and I promise to do the same for them."

You can switch up the script and include incentives or "bonus cash" to get the client to give out your cards. You can mix and match as you see fit. Your best bet is to test different ways out. You will get more comfortable as you ask more.

Client—Approach #2

When the time comes, you can spring a "surprise" help:

"John, we had that great conversation last week about upgrading to QuickBooks Online. I know you were worried about getting your team up to speed and I can help.

You're one of my top clients and my goal is to find more clients like you, so this might be helpful for you. I will train your entire team on QuickBooks Online, with five sessions over five weeks, absolutely free. All I ask is for three quality introductions to other people who might need the same help as you. How does that sound?"

Competitor Referral Trick

"Hi John,

I'm about to send a great prospect over to you. Right now, I'm not able to take them on, but knew you would take good care of them. I'm thinking there will probably be more of these coming soon and I'm happy to send them over to you.

Doing this again and again could put you in an uncomfortable spot as you might feel you need to reciprocate. I don't want you to feel that way at all. In the past, I've set up a "referral fee" arrangement with other partners where our firm would get a flat fee for every new client you sign based on one of our referrals.

Every time I send you a new client who needs help, I'll receive a finder's fee of $X,XXX." How does that sound?"

You could use this same script for any complementary vendor partners, such as lawyers or financial planners. It's a great way to add a bit more revenue without any effort.

Interviews to Go Deeper

1. Turn Contacts into New Clients - with David Fisher (https://jetpackworkflow.com/networking-for-accounting-clients-david-fisher/)

2. Build a Referral-Based Firm - with Michelle Long (https://jetpackworkflow.com/build-a-referral-based-cpa-firm/)

3. Working with the Best Clients Only - with Steve Pipe (https://jetpackworkflow.com/finding-freedom-firm-interview-steve-pipe/)

4. Become an Advisor for Clients - with Shelley Johnson (https://jetpackworkflow.com/become-an-advisor-clients-cpa-firm/)

5. Building a 7-Figure Firm - with Darren Root (https://jetpackworkflow.com/building-a-7-figure-firm-the-darren-root-interview/)

6. Two Simple Techniques to get More Referrals (https://jetpackworkflow.com/2-simple-techniques-get-referrals-accountants-bookkeepers/)

7. How to ask for a Referral from Clients (https://jetpackworkflow.com/how-to-ask-a-client-for-referrals/)

Recommendations

I started out on this career path for many years as an accountant at a CPA firm, before realizing my true love was writing sales copy and marketing. Once you get the client, you could bear more fruit just from referrals themselves.

Implementing these referral steps can seem overwhelming, so it's easy to just put them aside for another day.

From experience with prior clients, "another day" turns into another year and beyond. The fastest way to get your firm growing faster, finding the right clients, and increasing your income is to work alongside someone who already helps other companies get the clients they want.

As a free bonus for being a reader of this book, you get access to:

- A layout of personalized ideas for your firm to start growing your ideal client base. It's typically a 10–20-page document personalized for your company.

- A free initial consult that includes ideas and steps you can take right away (valued at $500). You will leave the call with the first steps to implementing the right system for your firm.

- A free trial for a short marketing project. Your first project, up to a certain size, will be 100% free. While many projects can run into the five-figures, your first project with me will have no charge, so you can be comfortable without risking any capital.

To get started, email me at joe@jccopy.com with the subject line "Let's Rock This." I read every email.

Chapter 6

Recruiting and Retaining Top Talent

I've heard this story many times. Diana's in the middle of building the "firm of the future." She's built a core team around herself. One day, her top accounting manager walks into her office, plops a resignation letter on her desk and gives notice.

She didn't see any warning signs. Everyone seemed happy…

With financial recruiters, LinkedIn, and easy access to job listings, keeping top talent around can be one of the hardest things for a growing firm.

Every day, firm owners feel stranded or under-resourced when recruiting top talent. Bigger firms pay more and offer more mobility, so they can often be more attractive to quality employees. When a small firm finally does hire someone excellent, they leave after a year or two, *just when everything was starting to click.*

You've heard it's more expensive to hire someone new than to keep old talent, and it's true. The landscape for recruiting has never been more challenging and for those firms who sit outside a major hub, it can be even more challenging to keep a pipeline of candidates coming through the doors.

As you grow, your process and team should be the constants. Making yourself a "career firm" leads to faster implementation of these steps, better corporate culture, and more profits. Every time a manager gets recruited to another firm because of money, you know there's something wrong.

When we zoom out of the industry, it's not only higher salaries that keep employees. We see people of all ages leave one company for another that offers less pay and we also see people stay at a job that offers less pay when they could be making much more somewhere else. Simply put, pay isn't the only thing people care about.

Of course, we're assuming that the compensation you give is adequate to meet a certain standard of living. Beyond that, the modern workforce is full of individuals who care about more than just a 3% pay raise.

Because bigger firms have deeper pockets, they might be able to provide travel opportunities and they give a CPA a brand name to put on their résumé. So for a smaller firm like yours, it can seem daunting to rally the troops and keep your employees happy with other firms knocking at the door.

But it's not as difficult as you might think.

As the younger generation starts to make up more and more of the workforce, there is a huge opportunity for your firm. These younger CPAs care about your mission and your culture, and they care about enjoying where they work. They want their opinions heard, their ideas explored, and someone who can mentor them. Larger firms say they can do all of this, but they simply cannot.

Because of their size, larger firms run like a well-oiled machine and young CPAs quickly get squeezed into the role of being nothing more than a cog. As your firm grows, you can offer something these larger firms can't. *Flexibility.*

Flexibility, especially with younger CPAs, gives an intangible benefit to working with your firm rather than a Big 4. In order to keep growing and doubling your revenue, you need to keep the talent steady, growing, and happy. It's your legacy you're building.

Your succession plan should be a priority. It would be best to nurture and grow your future from the bottom, up. But more and more, partners are actually being recruited into smaller firms. This will warn new talent coming into the firm that there is a problem on the team management front.

You can see it on their website. If a handful of their partners only recently joined the firm in the past few years, it's a sign there's something wrong. Partners act as the generals and captains of the firm. In sports, they would be the coaches calling the shots. The more time the coaches and players have together, the better communication gets, and the more success they see.

Look at your own firm right now. Do you have a solid set of partners grown from the bottom? Do you have managers prepared to take the next step in five years? Are your CPA practitioners enthusiastic about the future and not simply making a pit stop at your firm, intending to head to another firm in the near future?

Now, I'm not saying you're going to have zero turnover. It's virtually impossible to manage that and you will take those bumps and bruises as they come. However, you can trim turnover more and more if you focus at the very start of the relationship: find the right talent and sort through them to find long-term employees.

It is tempting to simply fill in the holes as more clients rush through the door or as tax season kicks off. That's what most firms do; they quickly bring in a handful of interns or hire the first CPA they interview. Only later do they find out the person was an awful fit.

They end up making excuses like, *"But, I needed the body to do the work."*

It's about survival and I understand that. Sometimes you just need a Band-Aid. But as you implement these pillars, you will likely open up capacity and need fewer employees. Or you might get aggressive with your marketing and need to hire more.

As a rule of thumb, it's better to over-hire the right people than rush and hire the wrong people. Again, hiring a new employee is much more expensive than you think when you factor in recruiting fees, training, administrative costs to set up accounts, sign-on bonuses, and technology set up. But when you over-hire great people, at least you know everyone there will stick with it for the long haul.

A new hire can also slow down work efficiency. Managers and practitioners must stop their daily tasks to meet and train the new hire, thus eating up capacity. But when you hire the right people who fit in with your culture, you don't have to worry about constantly hiring. Along with that, you enjoy a host of benefits, including:

- Increased profits as employees become more efficient over time.
- A steady, enjoyable culture of long-term employees.
- A succession plan you can lean on.
- Happier clients who feel secure as they aren't shuffled between team members.
- Closer relationships between team members, which creates a more positive and attractive work environment.

In the sections below, we'll outline how some firms have built a pipeline of highly qualified, hungry candidates, while others struggle, regardless of location.

We'll highlight owners who brought a team together under a common vision, and who retain and support those employees through ongoing, cost effective training and investments back into their team.

Our hope is that this chapter can expand your vision for your firm and give you some insights into why people join or stay at specific firms.

However, although we will get into specific *tactics*, do not ignore the *principles* in these pages. If you nail the principles, the tactics can shift and change as necessary. For example, we might highlight a firm owner who allows their team to watch March Madness, even though it's the middle of tax season, because they value a relaxed, enjoyable, and fun atmosphere. Others might want a more disciplined, rigid environment with extremely well-dressed employees and to-the-point, highly efficient work. Both approaches are fine, as long as you consciously make these decisions and hire people who will fit into that culture.

In the following pages, we'll dive into building your mission, vision, and values, as well as how to incentivize, reward, manage, communicate with, and invest in your team.

Problems with Retention and the Increase in Financial Recruiters

I was chatting with a financial recruiter recently and discovered a disturbing trend. Normally, a recruiting firm has one arm and a batch of clients they regularly help fill roles for. It's a faux pas to recruit a person that they have previously helped place.

For example, if Firm A is a client to the recruiting firm and Firm B comes along needing a new CPA, it would be bad faith for the recruiting firm to dip into Firm A to fill the position, even if there's a great fit. That's the standard.

The recruiting firm I talked with, however, had found a loophole. They had acquired and started a handful of firms. In their office, you can tell they are all under the same umbrella, but looking at them online, you can't.

These firms would pull what is called the fishbowl. One fish would jump out of one bowl into the other, and right after, a different fish would jump into the first bowl. So, Firm A loses a CPA to Firm B. Firm B had an opening because a CPA left for Firm C. Firm C had an opening because a CPA just left for Firm A.

Confusing, right?

Essentially, the recruiting firms, in order to keep their hands clean, would cross-pollinate. But they did it in a way to keep good faith. They have three recruiting firms cross-pollinating with each other and collecting commission checks on all three transactions.

Right when the CPA in Firm A wants to move, a recruiter contacts CPAs in Firms B and C to drum up interest in Firm A. Then, the process begins.

These recruiters pull in massive commissions; typically 10–35% of a candidate's first-year salary. To do the numbers, if a CPA's salary is $60,000, a recruiting firm can earn up to $20,000 for a single placement. With the fishbowl technique, that balloons to $60,000 or more!

Recruiters, with the dawn of LinkedIn, can now make contact with team members in a variety of ways. They can be as shameless as calling up your office and getting the team member on the phone to pitch.

So, why is this important?

Because in the past, most people graduated from college, got a job, and spent their 40-year career in that one position, regardless if they enjoyed the work.

Now, younger workers buck this trend. Many millennials job-hop every two years, as they get bored at a position. These financial recruiters know this and lick their chops at the gold lying in wait.

In the past, you could get away with letting culture slide. No one was quitting anyway. But times are different now. Candidates expect to be wooed. They expect a position where they can share ideas, no matter if they just graduated from college and know little about the industry.

This younger generation, whether you like it or not, are the future of your firm and of the legacy you created. You cannot expect younger CPAs to behave and learn exactly as you did. You must adapt.

Retention remains one of the hardest pieces of the puzzle in this decade. No more can you sit idle, strolling around the office with a "do as I say and no questions asked" attitude, neglecting to build trust with future leaders.

Remember when you first started out? You knew little and probably made many mistakes. At some point, you may have had a firm partner take you under their wing, motivate you, push you to do better, and lay the bricks leading to a partnership.

There's more stress in the life of the working person than ever before. You already juggle pending deadlines, a family at home, friends outside the office, plus your hobbies. Taking care of your team is always a "wait until later" line on the firm checklist, but the reality is that you should make it a priority starting today.

This chapter focuses on building up your company culture and investing in your employees. It's sixth, not because it's less important, but because it's the one that takes the longest to implement and see results.

Molding leaders for your future takes months, then years. It's an ongoing process you need to revisit each quarter. Every time someone leaves, ask why. Instead of getting frustrated with the person leaving and shunning them, as many firms do, sit down and have an open and honest discussion.

Then sit down with current team members and openly ask, *"John, I ask this not to intrude, but to learn. Have you had recruiters reach out to you about positions?"*

If they say "No," they are lying and that's a whole other issue. Even starting bookkeepers get solicited. When you hear "Yes," dig into what kind of offers appeared attractive and which didn't.

Teach them to listen to recruiter pitches and discover ideas of what other firms are doing that might be interesting for your firm. It's much like sending someone behind enemy lines, but you can learn so much. When you give a team member the freedom to entertain other offers and gather ideas, you build trust with that team member.

It's dangerous as you don't want to come across as though you don't care if they leave. Absolutely not. You need to make sure you approach it as though you want you to find ideas to implement so they enjoy working at your firm more. That's the difference.

In the past, finding a new job required scouring through the newspaper and even mailing in résumés. Now, you can have a bad day at work, go home, fire up a job board, message a recruiter, send out a few résumés, and get called the next day to interview.

It's so easy and it's dangerous for firm owners. These things happen every day, but it's not because of just one bad day. It comes from a team member not understanding their importance, not feeling appreciated, and not being given the freedom they crave to explore their strengths.

Joe, the co-author of this book, was an accountant and almost-CPA for many years. He ventured out into helping financial companies with their marketing because of his interest in the area and his lack of options at the companies he was working for. He says:

> *"I grew up wanting to be an accountant, for some odd reason. I loved numbers and the role of a CFO. After working in accounting for a few years, I realized I enjoyed the financial space, but not so much doing the day to day grind in QuickBooks. On top of that, I actually wasn't very good at it, so I approached the VP asking if I could try focusing on business development, instead.*

> *Only a few people at the firm focused on BD, but most new clients came from referrals. The firm wanted to double growth in the next few years, so I saw this as an opportunity to use my strengths in marketing. I had been doing work on the side for a while, so I knew I could add value to the firm that way, as I wasn't much of an accountant.*

> *I was essentially told "No," and to keep my head down in QuickBooks. Eventually, I left to work for myself. Many owners reading this might think, "Everyone can't just do what they want, there would be chaos," and I agree with that, but seeing there was little BD going on, a nearly non-existent marketing team, and the goal to grow fast, I felt entertaining new ideas would do more good than harm.*

> *I was told, since I wasn't a veteran in the CPA world, my ideas wouldn't be taken seriously. If I had felt heard and given a shot, I would probably still be at that firm."*

There's a stigma in firms that the oldest know best. Younger folks enter firms that preach being "entrepreneurial," only to be hushed and pushed back into their cubicles. Top companies such as Google and Amazon get ideas from all branches of hierarchy every day. Much of what you see of Google was thought up and built from those at the bottom.

So, why would CPA firms be any different? Just because a partner has been there for 40 years doesn't mean they understand what's happening in the market today.

Retaining top talent goes far beyond a steady paycheck and bumps in job title. It needs to include the intangibles. Employees must be aligned with your mission and your values. Any incongruence will stand out and cause an exodus that will result in even more turmoil.

Let's change that.

Forming a Culture

What keeps you coming back to work each day?

For your employees, the answer will probably start with money. For firms who have built the right culture, you'll hear other things like sense of purpose, vision, and passion.

When you give someone a strong "why" for what they do, it keeps them going. Your culture forms when you have the right "why" in place for each member of your team.

Stephen King, the CEO of GrowthForce, says, *"There is a culture intentionally built, or reactively built."*

Giving employees a strong "why" for being at their desk everyday takes effort. If you simply let the culture form "naturally," you can run into problems.

We already discussed that, in the past, workers tended to remain at jobs even if they didn't enjoy it in order to appear responsible. They often felt like they owed the company for giving them a shot in the first place. Over generations, the landscape has changed, making your culture paramount. You must make active strides to mold the culture you wish to form.

Early in your firm's life, the culture was built based on the original founder(s) and employees. As more people joined the firm, the culture may have stayed the same or shifted a bit, but the culture that resulted was a reaction to changes in the population and the field. The important thing, now, is to grab the reins and control it, creating an intentional culture that will make your current CPAs love working at your firm and stay with you for as long as possible.

Dramatic, reactive shifts could scare off your future leaders and that could come from just one or two bad hires. It's shaky ground you walk on every time you introduce a new face.

To start formulating the right culture, you must begin with your vision, mission, and core values.

Vision

Your vision lays out the dreams of your firm. What type of firm do you want? What types of clients are best?

You defined the scope of this while you built your ideal client and USP. Your vision builds on those pieces.

- How big do you want to grow?
- Do you want to expand into another state?
- What roles should each employee strive for?
- What does the firm look like in 10–20 years?

Your vision is the dream you started out with when you first started. It should be what motivates employees to want to change the processes and to market the firm More, ask for referrals, stick around, and not jump ship.

"You want everyone who walks in the door to understand how their behaviors and actions fit into the company's goals and vision. If you haven't laid out the goal, you're 70–80% there just by writing it down. It's your three-year painted picture."

–Stephen King

Each employee, when you hire them, must understand your vision and what their part is in it. Your vision must inspire everyone to work toward that goal and must focus on something that will matter to your employees. If your vision is to grow large enough to sell to a Big 4 firm and retire young, your team, unless they have equity, will not be motivated to partake.

Let's look at an example outside the industry: Amazon.com, the largest online marketplace. This is their vision statement:

"Our vision is to be earth's most customer centric company; to build a place where people can come to find and discover anything they might want to buy online."

When Amazon hires new employees, they should want to build the vision of a global marketplace, as well. That's how Amazon can continue to work toward their vision and create a culture around it.

For those who love working at Amazon, they are proud that their company leads the world in ecommerce. They keep coming to work because they believe Amazon does ecommerce better than anyone else and they will only get better the next 10–20 years.

Google gets thousands of applicants each year. I would estimate most want to work there because, besides fortune and prestige, they see

Google changing the world with what they build. Who wouldn't want to be a part of a company that changes the world?

With your firm, you need to construct your vision to fit what your current team already believes in and ensure that future hires accept and enthusiastically participate in working toward that goal as well.

To build your vision:

1. Think about what you want to be known for.
2. Understand how you want to be "game-changers" in the industry.
3. Know what makes your firm unique and special. (Think USP.)

A local firm in Vermont might have the vision of being the go-to firm in the Northeast for all construction companies. Owners come to them to grow financially so they can build more.

It's simple, but has a direct purpose. It's also a vision a new hire can understand and see as achievable. Simply saying: *"We want to be the best CPA firm around..."* doesn't resonate, as it's vague and uninspiring.

A vision like the one above, would attract other CPAs who have worked in the construction industry and want to leave a mark. They've found a firm who has a vision that aligns with their skillset.

Sit down, not with just the partners, but your whole team. What would inspire them? What goal do they want to see you achieve? What do you want to be known for?

Once you define your vision, you can then add your mission statement to it.

Mission

Your mission goes hand-in-hand with your vision for the company. The mission simply asks, "Why?"

- Why did you start this company?
- Why does your company exist?

Remember, your vision looks ahead to what you want the firm to be in the future, so your mission should delve into why that's important.

An example of a mission statement for a firm might be:

> *We seek to reinvent small business accounting so no one reverts back to old accounting practices.*

This founder may have seen so many firms living in the past in how they do accounting—some still use paper and pencil…—and wanted business owners to have the most efficient methods as possible.

You, or the founder, must have had a reason for starting the firm. Of course, there will be underlying reasons, such as owning your own business, but there will also be things you felt you could do better than everyone else. I hear these types of stories all the time on the podcast.

I started Jetpack Workflow (https://jetpackworkflow.com/) because CPA firms weren't efficiently tracking their work, because the processes were outdated and broken. Jetpack makes sure every one of your accounting clients gets 100% of the work they paid for, on time.

At the construction CPA firm, they might have thought, *"We seek to give construction owners a less stressful business and personal life where all their projects are funded and employees get paid on time."*

That second portion is the "Why." The mission.

Think about the personal story behind your firm. Consider the issues you help your clients with and the services you offer that they thank you over and over again for. What you do best for your clients—deeper than just completing a tax return—becomes your mission.

Again, you can peel a bit off from the marketing lessons in Chapters 3, 4 and 5. Listening to your clients gives you subtle hints about your mission. Whenever you feel fulfilled in your work, that's a good sign you've completed your mission successfully in that instance.

This takes some time to wrap your head around. Sit down with different members of your team and get their ideas on the mission. Find similarities and you'll eventually find your main purpose.

Then, tying in your vision with your mission can help you point out the core values you look for in a team member. That's what we will look at next.

Core Values

Core values is a business jargon phrase; many people use it but few understand it. Your core values are the way you conduct yourself and run the practice.

Here are some examples of good and bad core values practices:

- **Bad core values:** Arthur Andersen made a fortune auditing the books of Enron. They neglected their processes and standard auditing practice in order to maximize their profits.
- **Good core values:** A firm declines to take an equity position in a client due to the conflict of interest that might occur.

On your team, your new hires and team members are your *"how."* Your "how" is your core values.

- How do you go into battle and conquer your vision?
- How do you rally around a mission?

You have a team.

Much like a car, each piece of your team has a vital function. If one part doesn't work, the rest of the car will break down. If you put the wrong oil and gasoline in the tank, the car may run for a bit, but at some point, you will run into problems.

When you've built the right team, everything runs smoothly. If you rush to fix a solution, you risk putting the wrong fuel in your tank. It may work out for a bit, but sooner rather than later, problems will come to light.

Look at your top partners and team members. What do they all have in common? What should all new hires have?

Going back to Stephen King, CEO of GrowthForce, he hires "behaviors, not skills." Skills can be taught over time, but behaviors are normally ingrained in a person.

A core value you could look for in team members should be that they, *"Work and learn fast—they accomplish this because they find a deeper meaning in what they do."*

For this example, your employees should want people to pick up the work fast, not because they have the skillset, but because they discover the importance of the work they are doing.

Paula Allgood, Managing Partner at Beaird Harris & Co., believes her firm's core values are to "attract people who get a charge out of the work and want to grow within the firm."

For Paula's firm, she wants people who live and breathe accounting and can see themselves as a partner in a CPA firm for the rest of their career, rather than treating this job as a stepping stone to a CFO position elsewhere.

You need to figure this out before you hire anyone else. What are the core *behaviors* you want already instilled in each candidate who walks through the door?

No, you don't want everyone to be the same. We aren't talking about personality. Personality is a smaller slice in terms of fitting in the social culture. In terms of work culture, everyone should have similar traits. If your core values are that you live and breathe accounting, are a fast learner, and are fluid with your learning, then you should be hiring employees that meet those standards.

Whatever is working for your firm now, that's probably the answer. If it's not where you want it, think about what makes sense for your firm. Every firm will be different.

Armed with these three cultural foundation points, you can walk into an interview with a candidate and find the one you are looking for. You'll know if they will fit into your company culture, and if they will be motivated to work toward your vision.

Hiring the Right Staff

When you understand what you need out of a new team member, it's much easier to sift through candidates. For most firms, you live and die by who the recruiter brings through the door. You might get a few applications online, but you're never sure if the candidate would be a good fit.

Your vision, mission and core values should be at the heart of your interview with each applicant. You need to see each new hire as *the* future of your firm. If you feel this person isn't here to make a statement and grow the firm, go with your gut. That person isn't for you.

You can't afford to be like so many firms who hire someone as fast as possible to deal with work overflow. You're better off contracting a temporary employee to handle that, rather than bringing in a full-time hire if you aren't 100% sure who or what you are looking for.

Chet Buchman, Managing Partner at Swindoll, Janzen, Hawk & Lloyd, CPA, actually recommends overstaffing during busy times. He says, *"Hire ahead of the busy curve."*

If you see a great potential fit for your firm, go for it even if you aren't necessarily hiring. Using the pillars in this book, you will enjoy more capacity but also more clients, because you'll be growing. Eventually you will need this person and you don't want to find out months later that they now work for your competitor.

It can be tricky to figure out a new candidate. Obviously, they are on their best behavior at this point. It's up to you to find the forest for the trees. Look back at your core values and ask the candidate to tell stories of their work. Find those clues to tie into your values.

Finding the right employee can be tough, so here are a few things you want to make sure you learn about your potential hire during the interview:

- What motivates them. Is it growth? Learning? Autonomy?
- How they spend their free time. This gives you a glimpse at the candidate's personal *"why."* If they aren't growing in their free time, they probably aren't looking to grow with you.
- How they solve problems. Does it mesh with your culture?
- The kind of work culture they came from. It's probably the culture they want to avoid.
- How they interact with clients. Ask about a story of working with a client.

Paula Allgood, to cut to the heart of it and find behaviors, not skillsets, gives new candidates a few personality tests. These include:

- Kolbe Test: A personality test based on instinct. Reviewing the results, you learn about your *conative* abilities. In other words, how they act in specific situations. This is one test that's becoming more common to use in the interview process.
- StrengthsFinder Test: An aptitude test in which you and your candidate learn their top five strengths. As a firm owner, you can compare these to the rest of your team to see if they would be a good fit.

The tests, Paula says, allows you to get an idea of how a person works and how they might work with other members of your team. What works is that the tests don't focus as much on their skills, but on their personality and what they would enjoy. You can get a better idea of whether or not the candidate would mesh with your current team and your client roster.

Chad Ridner, Founder of Two Roads, believes team members need to enjoy their work, their clients, and their teammates. If one of these is off, it can throw off your culture.

When hiring at his firm, he gives two different competency tests to make sure the basic skills are there and then follows up with, at minimum, four face-to-face interviews. Having different team members interview with the candidate allows various opinions and that data can lead to a better decision. Your team can determine the talent fit and the cultural fit. You need to determine this before even discussing compensation issues.

When it comes to compensation, you need to figure out the motivation for the candidate. Is compensation one of the main motivators or is it just a perk or necessity to them? Are there other ways your employees would like to be compensated?

Many firms approach compensation as just salary, but you can get creative and add in other types of compensation as well. There are many different forms of compensation, so here are just a few suggestions:

- Cross-train them in various positions as a bonus so they don't get bored and can broaden their skillset.
- Provide paid training to the candidate and even tickets to conferences they would enjoy.
- Give them autonomy on certain one-off projects they can pick.
- Pay for a professional development or educational program they can participate in. For example, a 12-week leadership course.
- Provide a slight bump in bonuses for retirement and for performance.

Chris Ragain, Managing Director of Ragain Financial, gives a candidate a five-year look ahead for what the candidate will make in salary. It gives them something to look forward to, plus a closer insight on what to expect going forward.

The more value you can put into an offer, the less a candidate focuses on salary and sees the bigger picture.

Once you get the candidate to accept, you must now start to nurture, retain, and motivate them.

Retaining and Motivating Employees

This is the most neglected step of the hiring process. The wooing of a candidate doesn't stop at the interview, anymore. You can no longer expect your employees to stick around. Remember, it's as easy as ever to pick up and switch jobs. Firms are getting used to high turnover, but that doesn't have to be the case for you.

Retaining employees requires concrete steps and a concentrated effort. It's easy to focus on work and finding new clients, but treating your clients best starts with treating your team well.

As your company grows, a framework needs to be put in place to move new hires into the fold. One of my friends, Jack, went through a lengthy interview process. Throughout, he got to chat with the partners individually for a while and really clicked with them. He signed the deal and looked forward to learning from them.

Unfortunately, that's not how it turned out. Jack got pushed into his cubicle, placed under a manager, and now the most he gets from the partners is a quick nod in the breakroom.

His excitement and one of the main reasons he joined the firm—to learn under experienced partners—didn't come to fruition. Last I checked, he's looking around for another position.

So, to keep your employees happy, you must figure out what motivates them and create a plan around it.

Determining if a Team Member is Engaged

I get it, you can't follow every employee around everywhere and it doesn't need to be that way to ensure they remain engaged. You can do things once a month to keep employees engaged. In that same stretch, you will still want to maintain the culture.

Your culture forms from the mission, vision and core values laid out, which brings in a certain breed of CPAs and creates the culture at your firm.

You will run into problems when a team member doesn't mesh with the culture. If someone doesn't, it typically goes right back to these three pieces:

- Does the team member feel they are part of a vision, and are they excited about it?
- Does the team member work at the Firm for the reason our mission states?
- Does the team member match the core values we look for in a candidate?

I guarantee if someone is not fitting in well, it's because one of these points are off. This leads to the question, *when do I let someone go?*

Obviously, letting go of anyone is a tough decision. It can be costly and make other team members fear for their own position.

Normally, bad fits tend to work themselves out of the firm at some point, again, it's easy to switch jobs due to recruiters. I would recommend letting someone go only if they are destroying your culture completely. If that's not the case, it might be easiest to simply nudge the team member towards a different role.

Letting go of a team member is a tough situation and is unique for each firm, thus I won't dive much more into it. You need to weigh your options on what makes the most sense and if there are more pros than cons when it comes to letting them go.

Rather than having to face removing a team member for not fitting in with the culture, the next best solution is finding new ways to motivate and energize them. Your team might love the work they do, but not enjoy where they do it. Just as you can love ice cream, but not want to eat it while hiking through Antarctica. But then, in the 100+ degree heat of the desert, that same ice cream suddenly tastes and feels incredible.

Steps to Motivate and Retain

Your team will love what they do even more when in the right circumstances, so the decision remains: what are you going to do to motivate and retain your employees?

Chet Buchman knows. No one wants to spend their 30-year career behind a desk. Employees are now looking for more from companies, but some firms are still catching up with this idea. Employees won't just show up and accept unhappiness, so it's up to you to accept this cultural shift in the workplace.

Here are 12 ideas you can implement right away:

1. **Work together at setting goals around their needs:** Each employee has a vision for themselves and how they fit into

the firm. They may not want to become a partner due to the time constraints. The position of manager may work better for them. Find ways to help them towards those goals.

2. **Provide flexible work hours:** It's becoming more common to work from home and outside the office. Working from home is proven to reduce stress and increase employee happiness.

3. **Encourage them with regular positive feedback:** Be generous with positive feedback. Give praise in front of others. Drop a $10 Starbucks gift card from time to time with a note.

4. **Create bite-sized, manageable goals:** For each project, organize it into small steps they can accomplish quickly to stay motivated and feel accomplished.

5. **Create interactive games:** Pick a random Friday and organize a scavenger hunt for the firm. Get people interacting with each other. Some other ideas include: Bingo Wednesdays or mini-golf Fridays.

6. **Take your accountants out individually:** Give them one-on-one time with you. This could be just twice a year, but it will leave a major impact with your team members.

7. **Radiate positivity:** Be the first one smiling each day, especially during stressful times. Don't show up to Casual Friday in a suit.

8. **Be the open door:** Every few days, stop at different team members' desks and say hi.

9. **Let your accountants lead:** Give your team members chances to be in the spotlight and show off their expertise.

10. **Offer cash:** Money always helps! Surprise them on tax day with a $100 gift card to Amazon.

11. **Plan an outdoors day:** How about a day at the bowling alley or driving range? That'll mix it up!

12. **Give a surprise day or week off:** You don't need to give away cash to boost morale. Simply email the team on Friday to, *"Take Monday off, see you Tuesday."* I promise your production will remain steady.

Figure out what type of culture you want to create. If you a family-first firm, set mandatory "leave" hours or limit maximum work hours.

If you are a fun firm, implement Happy Hour Thursdays at lunch.

You choose, with your mission statement, the direction you want to head. Then, look at your current team and discuss with them what they want to see change in the firm.

Paula Allgood's firm wanted to give a more relaxed atmosphere, so with the office remodel, they installed a community workstation along with two flat screen televisions. During tax season, CPAs can fill out 1040s while rooting for their college during March Madness.

Chet Buchman's firm implemented a 15-minute reading rule, before you do your work. It's optional, but over 90% of the firm participated. It started simply because they realized the first minutes of the workday are unproductive. Now, they start the day with non-work related activities, such as 15 minutes of non-fiction reading, to get the day going.

Could you bring pets to work once a month? This is a tougher proposition, but international studies prove pets at work reduce overall stress and it's fun. I can't guarantee work will get done as efficiently, but remember, sometimes you need to focus on the intangibles to see more tangible results.

Use these ideas to start brainstorming what might work for your firm. Retaining and motivating your employees needs to be a top priority as you build your firm and expand your client base. Get input from your team members as well, since it is them you're trying to keep motivated and committed.

Conclusion

As younger CPAs enter the workforce, they expect more. No longer can you expect team members to put their heads down and work without complaints. Financial recruiters are forever on the prowl to snatch each one of your employees away. The reason? They get paid hefty fees to do so.

You must focus on your culture to keep employees engaged with your firm. To start building the right culture, you must create your vision, mission, and core values.

Your vision is what you see the firm being in the next 10–20 years. Your mission is *"why"* you are in business, and your core values are the ways you conduct yourself in how you act and perform your duties.

These three pieces cement the foundation for hiring your next staff member. It's after you hire that next employee, though, when the hard work to motivate and retain them begins. Talk with each team member to discover the best methods to keep your employees engaged and excited to be a part of your firm.

This can take time, effort, and probably some failure. Your firm is always a work in progress, but at least you are working toward your goals.

Action Steps

1. Define your vision, mission, and core values. Ask yourself, "Have we gotten input from all our team members?"

2. Examine your hiring process. Hint: look at your current team and turnover to evaluate if it's working.

3. Create an individual file for each employee so you can understand what drives them. Go over it at least twice a year.

4. Consider what you do to retain your culture. Does it need to change?

5. Develop a bonus structure you can implement that isn't necessarily based on money, but that could greatly boost your team culture and morale.

Interviews to Go Deeper

1. 3 Steps to Building an Effective Team - with Chad Ridner (https://jetpackworkflow.com/3-crucial-steps-to-building-an-effective-accounting-team/)

2. Transform Your Firm into a Profitable Powerhouse - with Paula Allgood (https://jetpackworkflow.com/transform-your-cpa-firm-into-a-profitable-powerhouse/)

3. Retain Top Talent with a Better Work/Life Balance - with Chet Buchman (https://jetpackworkflow.com/how-to-master-a-work-life-balance-program-within-your-firm/)

4. Building an All-Star Team - with Stephen King (https://jetpackworkflow.com/building-star-team-culture-stephen-king-interview/)

5. Working with Younger Talent in the Firm - with Sandra Wiley (https://jetpackworkflow.com/how-to-build-a-team-that-fuels-firm-growth-the-sandra-wiley-interview/)

6. Empower Team to Grow the Firm - with Angie Grissom (https://jetpackworkflow.com/creating-5-star-service-scaling-excellence-angie-grissom-interview/)

Recommendations

I've implemented much of this just building my own team here at Jetpack Workflow (https://jetpackworkflow.com/). If you have ideas on how to better motivate and inspire your team, send them over. I can share what I've learned with you, as well, from the many guests on my podcast.

Email me: david@jetpackworkflow.com

Chapter 7

How to Build Out New Profit Centers

This might be the only chapter that comes with a word of caution, especially for those owners who are prone to Shiny Object Syndrome: new profit centers are a privilege, not a foundational element. If you do not have your existing service fulfillment, team management, client acquisition, and workflow system in place, adding a new profit center will only compound any existing confusion and add stress to the firm's culture.

When we put together this book, we looked to prioritize what you need to be doing first. Your workflow and processes come first because it's paramount to seal the foundation before building on it. The last step you should take is to add profit centers. It shouldn't be done until you get the first six pillars handled and working.

We are about to dive into adding new profit centers to your business. The average millionaire has seven different income streams. An average American has one, sometimes two. That's the difference between massive wealth growth and living check-to-check.

Looking at your own firm, where do you stand? Are you skimping because the bulk of your revenue derives solely from tax returns and some QuickBooks work? You can grow a healthy firm this way, but we're focusing on growing your firm well beyond that.

Let me start with an example on the power of profit centers:

Every year, there's a viral article on how some celebrity spent hundreds of thousands of dollars on single night at a club. Typically, this fanfare and gossip column doesn't apply to your business, but in this case, it absolutely does.

Elite and exclusive clubs are masters of building profit centers. Think about a typical nightclub. What would they have to provide to make $1M in a weekend? Instantly, a few services come to mind:

- Special chauffeur and limo service
- VIP seating and bottle service
- High-end alcohol
- VIP access to the dance floor or behind the scenes with the DJ
- In-club gambling and sports betting
- Exclusive (and expensive) food offers

The point is not how much money a club can make, but rather their *mindset* about profitability. They know that even if only 5% of their customers purchase these upgrades they will build a significantly more profitable business than just running the average club. Profit centers in your firm have the same potential. In the following pages, we'll dissect some of the best new profit centers to launch in order to grow your business.

Look at Big 4 firms. They haul in billions each year, but it's not all from corporate tax returns. They have an audit division, a management consulting arm, assurance services, and they even help with raising and negotiating venture capital.

Now, the point isn't to turn you into a Big 4 firm. Rather, to steal some of the secrets they, and other successful firm owners, implement daily to build their revenue base.

As mentioned, if you don't get everything else right first, new profit centers will simply cause mass chaos. Your foundation must be set first.

We interviewed Mike Bark, Partner and Co-founder at EdgeAdvise, about adding profit centers. When Mike added his first one, he already had a solid foundation of accounting work in the niche he was targeting. He also had previously referred and worked with the individual who would eventually own the new profit center. You will hear more about this later.

But first, let's look at the other side of it.

Bill, an average firm owner, spent five years growing his firm. He had ventured out on his own when his last, medium-sized firm started going in, what Bill considered, the wrong direction. When he founded this firm, he pledged, *"We will do things the right way for our clients."*

The firm's focus was on dentists, and honing in on this niche made it much more attractive for dentists to work with him. Thus, his client base grew rapidly. Bill hired to fill in the stop gaps to keep work from slipping through the cracks. His workflow and processes were essentially held together with duct tape.

He was chatting with a dental client one afternoon and the client mentioned how he could get rid of more paperwork and have everything virtual. Bill saw this as a multi-million-dollar opportunity.

As usual in 2016, he'd read the success stories of founders who built an app and sold it for a fortune. Immediately, he contracted a software engineer and a design firm to carry out his plans. He had employees begin introducing this product to their clients.

Rather than focusing on the work that needed to get done, Bill put everything into developing his software. He was running ragged and his bank account was plunging toward zero.

Unfortunately, the process all came to a head when projects finally found their way through the cracks and into his clients' hands. The quality of the work was poor, and to top it all off, every project was past due. To save his company, Bill scrapped the app development and went back to his core services. With all the work and money spent, it took months to piece everything back together and regain the trust of his clients.

Bill did exactly what you shouldn't do. Rather than focusing on building his firm's foundation and then expanding services, he put all his eggs in one basket and forgot about the core work he was doing. Of course, this isn't necessarily what will happen, but you see what *could* happen if you try to expand before ensuring your foundation is solid.

That's an extreme example, so don't be scared away from adding new profit centers. Building an app requires much more capital and planning than adding something like CFO consulting or upselling a $97 DIY guide for tax planning.

It's important to make sure that any new profit center you're adding is one that:

- You know your clients absolutely want and need. Validate this through multiple client requests.
- You know of an individual who can lead the new profit center. If that person is you, then you must feel comfortable stepping away from your core services and have management or leadership in place to ensure growth while your focus is split.

- You've gone through the worst-case scenario and the new profit center, if it fails, will not dramatically impact your core business.

The reason this section comes with a warning is because firm owners who are often struggling, bored, or are trying to avoid the uncomfortable action they need to take will *escape into a new profit center.*

It's easy to get distracted and even discouraged. Media posts all these success stories of the 25-year-old firm owner living on a yacht and making millions.

If you need to escape from the uncomfortable, take a vacation. But for your business, be fully present. Do not try to escape into a new profit center because it seems glamorous. Develop one because it makes your clients more successful, and strategically, it makes sense for the firm.

Now I say all this because, as a business owner myself, I struggle with this. *New* is more often more exciting. I get it. But if you want to tackle a new project, be sure your firm is already a well-oiled machine. Remember, if your foundation cracks, the entire building begins to crumble.

Having said that, for those who have done the work and *who do* have a solid foundation, adding a profit center is a great way to increase revenue, market leadership, referrals, and cross-selling opportunities. For people like Mike Bark, adding new profit centers has dramatically accelerated their growth and we hope they can do the same for your firm.

In this chapter, we will dive into various profit centers you could add. Some may be complementary to what you already offer, others could be a completely new opportunity you've uncovered. We will walk through the first steps to take before venturing into a new profit center and look at the other end of the spectrum. Are there services or products you could cut out or outsource?

This can be fun when done right!

The last thing an entrepreneur wants to hear is "patience," but that is what separates the best from the failures. The "best" were disciplined and worked at building up their business using the right processes, while the "failures" tried doing many things all at once with weak processes.

If you've never watched *The Profit* on CNBC with Marcus Lemonis (CEO of Camping World), you should tune in. On the show, Marcus helps struggling businesses. He invests in them and turns them around. When the deal falls through, a good percentage of the time, it is due to the owner wanting to do things the same (wrong) way he/she always did it.

When rebuilding companies, Marcus focuses on 3 pillars:

- People
- Processes
- Products

We focus on these same pieces, but with a different spin. You need to work on your people and your process first before opening up new product lines.

Types of Profit Centers You Could Add

Fast food chains always want to recreate themselves. There are so many burger joints, they're hard to count. Taco Bell comes out with some new twist on a taco or burrito every month, it seems. They do these things for a reason. They want to:

- Differentiate themselves
- Find new, profitable products
- Add value for customers

A potential customer might not want a plain burrito, but sprinkle Doritos on it, hot sauces, five different kinds of cheeses, and it might change minds.

When you think of accounting services, you could be boxed into the mindset of accounting work. You do taxes, so perhaps you could add some bookkeeping and payroll reports. This is what most firms do, but that's not what you're limited to.

There are tons of different services and products you could offer to your clients and most require you to think outside the box. In this section, we will open you up to some new ideas and suggest several different profit centers you could add.

When you do a business tax return and offer to do their bookkeeping, you are providing a *complementary service*. It's not far out of the realm of what you already do, as they are linked in many ways.

In fast food, when you order a burger, you automatically think of fries and a drink. Those are complementary products. Then, when your fast food joint starts selling salads or ice cream or breakfast options, these are *new products*. They fit within the realm of previous offerings—they are still food—but they are more than just a burger and fries.

The restaurant's brand is a "burger joint," yet they now offer things you might not correlate with a burger joint, such as pancakes and eggs or salads. With your firm, you can start doing the same thing.

Chris Ragain, Managing Partner at Ragain Financial, started off his firm like many others, doing business and personal tax returns. Chris launched his wealth management services when he constantly heard his business clients talk about issues with investing and financial management.

Mike Bark combined his previous practice with a partner who focused on mergers and acquisitions in the dental industry. After they established a core practice, he noticed a lot of clients were asking about their brochure design, website, and marketing materials, so they convinced their designer to launch a marketing and design profit center within their firm. He built a marketing agency right inside his practice!

For your firm, it might be a wealth management arm, it could be speaking events at industry conferences, information products, or even a software product you've developed. These add *new services* that relate to your existing products and services, but that offer brand new income streams.

Now, your favorite greasy spoon has started adding Marvel characters to their menu to advertise a new movie. They advertise tickets to the show on their packaging and the kid's meal toy is a character, as well. Now, they are partaking in a *joint venture*. Basically, they are getting paid to advertise to their customers.

Most CPA firms won't do something like that, but they may participate in joint ventures when advertising their own firm. It can be complicated, but what we mean here is partnering with vendors. Back in Chapter 5, we brought up negotiating with vendors for commissions on referrals. The same concept applies here.

Consider which services you are not equipped to provide, but could make a small cut off of. For example, most of your clients might need insurance so you can find a third-party vendor to offer that service to them. They probably need ongoing legal consulting, so call up your lawyer buddy and make a deal. Even large companies will pay out commissions if you sign up clients for their service.

Joint ventures allow you to add value for your client because they need specific services you don't have. At the same time, you get paid for the network of excellent service providers you've built.

It's the easiest money you can make as a firm owner.

As you build your client base, these commissions can stack up. The best part is, it's fairly easy to do. You can just refer them in one call.

We will get to the steps for implementing in a bit, but first, let's define three more potential profit makers.

Going Up, Down, and Across

Let's keep it simple and stay focused on a fast food chain. You just learned about the various profit centers your favorite burger joint takes advantage of. Now, let's uncover how they get maximum profits out of these complementary, new, and joint venture products.

A restaurant knows what items are more profitable than others. With a burger joint, you would think the burger is the most profitable item, but actually, it's not. The drinks are the most profitable. In fact, the profit margin on that $1 soda is close to 500%! The burger is closer to 33% profit. The restaurant hopes you get the burger, then automatically order the fries and drink with it. It's why they bundle them together to make a meal.

The bundle automatically looks like a great value to the customer and the restaurant makes a large profit on it.

Jay Holmes, Founder of Blueback Accounting, says, *"When the value you give to your clients increases, so does the frequency of interactions with them."*

This is why many burger joints now have a value menu. You can buy a small burger for $1. They hope to increase the frequency of your visits or hope you tack on a $1 soda for 500% profit.

At times, you may need to push customers towards a complementary product like this. When you order a burger and they ask, *"Do you want fries with that?"* You just heard a *cross-sell*. It's adding complementary products and services to what you ordered.

Remember, fries and soda are complementary items to a burger. With your client, they may ask you to do their business return and that's it. Now, you must pick up the conversation like a fast food worker, *"Do you want your personal return done with that as well?"*

I love sales tips, so here's one: *If you act like it's an obvious choice for the prospect, they will probably say "Yes" just to feel OK about their decision and out of respect for your expertise. It's your tone of voice that gets the sale.*

You could be leaving buckets of money on the table by simply not offering complementary services. Use the sales tip above to start doing that.

These fast food restaurants then find ways to extract more value from you on each visit. After you order a Number One, you might be asked, *"Would you like to make it a large for $2?"*

This is an example of an *upsell*. They took your current option and tried to add more to it for a higher price. In your firm, you can use this same strategy. The key being to add more services, but you want to upsell the most profitable ones.

If you just signed a bookkeeping client and want to do their payroll as well, look at how much more profit you make as compared to the same amount of effort doing a different task.

In your firm, you could upsell:

- 24/7 access to a CPA
- Additional consulting time slots
- Membership in a mastermind you put together for other owners in the niche
- A quarterly "check-in"

These items can be massively profitable and require little extra work. To upgrade your Number One from a medium to a large requires little extra work, but adds an additional 50% in profit for the restaurant.

That's how you need to think about it.

What if you say, "No, thanks" to the upgrade to a large? The worker may then ask, *"No problem, how about a 50 cent apple pie to enjoy for dessert?"*

You just experienced a *downsell*.

David Cristello & Joe Cassandra

It's a new offering after a cross-sell or an upsell was offered but declined. Typically, it's a cheaper option, but still highly profitable. In your firm, a downsell might be:

- Instead of 24/7 access, they get an FAQ for $49.
- Instead of quarterly check-ins, it's a one-time tax strategy session at the end of the year.
- Instead of additional consulting, you offer a $97 DIY guide to tax planning for the year-end.

With persuasion, in general, most people do not like telling someone "No" over and over again. That's why having these downsells in your back pocket can prove profitable over the long haul as the client will just say "Yes" so they don't have to say "No."

Call it a Jedi mind trick.

Now that you have these in mind—complementary, new, and joint venture services and products—plus the ways to extract the most value of them— cross-sell, upsell, and downsell—you can now start exploring the steps you should take to include them in your current offerings.

Finding New Income Streams in Your Firm

Edi Osborne, Founder of MentorPlus, says: *"You can't differentiate yourself based on something everyone else already knows."*

If you go into the marketplace offering the same thing everyone else does, and there aren't any distinguishable differences, you blend in and fade away. Opening up new profit centers highlights your current services and adds some flavor on the side. In the end, it all goes back to adding value to the client, and it starts with listening to them and understanding their problems.

To start, you must first understand the client value chain. *What does a client purchase before, during, and after your engagement with them?*

Let's step outside of fast food for a second and look at Apple. Before buying an iPhone, a customer probably purchased movies, books, music, and other similar things. They probably owned an iPod or music player of some sort. Apple built the App Store, then introduced their iPhones as an upsell opportunity and sold the iPhone to people who had already purchased iPods and media from the App Store and iTunes.

iPhones were a great accessory. Rather than hauling around a bulky computer or laptop, people can now carry around their phone. Then, Apple realized they could take an iPhone and basically blow it up to a manageable tablet, now known as an iPad. They built out all these product lines based on the client value chain.

For your firm, what services could be added as an upsell or developed as a whole new product based on your client value chain?

Perhaps, before hiring a CPA firm, a business owner needs an interim CFO to handle the day-to-day bills. After that, they hire a firm to manage all their taxes and bookkeeping, after which, they might need guidance to grow their own investments or their business.

You already heard about Mike Bark. He launched a marketing firm inside his own practice. You also heard about Chris Ragain, who developed a wealth management branch on top of his accounting firm. They both understood their client's needs and the client value chain.

Now, take some time to understand your own. Complete the below exercise to uncover more about your client value chain.

List your current service offerings:

1.
2.
3.
4.
5.

Rank them in order of the amount of business they bring in:

1.
2.
3.
4.
5.

Now look at these top service offerings and see if there is more value you can offer around these services. Where can you upsell? Where can you add a complementary or new service?

These are the types of questions you need to know the answers to. The only way to find the answers is to ask your clients.

We've been through this before in other chapters. Talking with your clients, extracting their pains, and discovering new opportunities are the key to opening up new profit centers. These are the type of questions you can ask a prospect during the sales process or to a client over the phone:

- What are your top priorities in any given week?
- How do you accomplish those?
- How do you measure and track success?

- What about your business keeps you up at night?
- If you could wave a magic wand, what would be the perfect service for you and your accounting needs?
- Is there a product or service you've been looking for but haven't found?

Push clients. Get them to really think through it. "Tell me more" and "Why?" always fleshes out ideas.

You should come away from these conversations with a list of pain points they have and would love to solve. You might already provide the solutions, or you know what would solve the problem. They might not know some of the inefficiencies in their processes, so you could surprise them with a new solution to save them time and money.

Think about these as you sort through the pain points. Now, you move to the next step:

List potential products and services:

1.

2.

3.

4.

5.

Just because you list them doesn't mean you should start implementing. For each one, you need to scrutinize which ones would be most profitable and best for your firm. Find out:

- What's the financial investment required?
- What about your investment in time?
- What is the estimated timeframe to see a return on this?

- How many current clients would buy it?
- Does it support your core offerings?
- After talking with 10 clients, would they buy it?
- Could we find three early adopters?

Remember, you shouldn't take this lightly. Adding a new profit center takes time, money, and expertise. Put each new idea through the ringer to make sure it will work.

Only after you do this should you add it to your rotation. With each new product or service, you will need to practice upselling, cross-selling, and downselling in order to present it to your client in the best way possible.

Don't leave any idea unexplored. Think about various information products to add, referral partners to introduce, CPA services to top off others. You want these to be high-profit pieces.

The more expertise you build up, the more your clients trust you and will be willing to invest with you.

Trim Services?

While we discuss *adding* profit centers, it's also a great idea to think about *removing* some of your offerings. You are bound to find a few of your services that are not profitable and that don't add value for your client. Perhaps these offerings are even negatively affecting your team.

It can be tempting to not say *"no"* to a client because you don't want to make waves. You may feel you are doing a great job by helping, but it may not be the case. For example, for some firms, doing client quarterly payrolls can be an unprofitable project. It can take more time and material cost than a client is willing to pay. Thus, you do it for them as a way to build goodwill with the client.

At some point, you need to measure how profitable doing payroll for a client really is. If you are only making 10% profit on it and not seeing any extra business, you might be better off getting rid of it.

I know of one firm that disliked doing 1099s for clients at year-end. Time would accumulate as team members tracked down EINs, addresses, the correct forms, and all the other information they needed. The problem was they couldn't bill out all the time because then it would be a $400 1099 and the client would be outraged. Thus, they had to offer the service for next to nothing while it cost the firm quite a lot to complete.

At some point, the firm needed to decide if it was worth it to keep offering this service. Did they want to be spending time with low-profit services like this? Was it time to tell clients they wouldn't be doing it anymore?

To start the process of trimming your services, list everything you offer. Consider which ones bring in the *least* amount of profit for the firm. Take away points from those your team members hate doing, as well. You might realize you've been propping up unprofitable services with your profitable ones all these years.

Your new profit centers should bring in high profit margins. Your core services, such as tax returns and bookkeeping might not be the highest profit builders, but they are the gateway to your more profitable ones.

Remember fast food restaurants. Burgers are less profitable than their complementary products. Your complementary services should not be lower or at the same profit level as your core products. If that's the case, you need to remove them.

Cell phone carriers, such as Verizon and AT&T, don't make much profit when they sell iPhones and Androids out of their stores. They make most of their profit on the plans and fees they charge each month. Their phone offerings bring clients to the door, but it's the plans that make the money.

Go through your complementary and new services. Which ones aren't profitable? Consider getting rid of them to make room for more profitable ones.

Conclusion

A new profit center could be an exciting prospect for your firm. You may even see dollar signs in your dreams. None of those dreams will come to pass if you don't set your foundation first. Make sure you have an efficient workflow and the right team before expanding into new profit centers.

As business owners, we want to dive into each new idea with reckless abandon. Successful businesspeople look like they do this, but actually they go through hundreds of ideas before executing just one. It takes patience and discipline on your part. Your team relies on you to make smart, profitable decisions.

Each new profit center needs to be vetted to the max. You should test each one with a handful of clients before rolling it out and spending more money to develop it.

As you think about developing new profit centers, you first need to pick a type of product or service, complementary, new, or joint venture.

Complementary goes hand-in-hand with your core offerings. New offerings can be something completely different, such as a software application, and a joint venture could simply be referring out to third-party vendors and getting a slice of the revenue.

Once you decide on a type, you then need to maximize the value of all your offerings with cross-sells, upsells, and downsells.

Cross-sells simply tack on a complementary offering to what the client already ordered. Upselling pushes a client to get added services that might not be core offerings on their own, but are high value. Downselling acts as a last-ditch effort when a client turns down the cross-sell and upsell. It's still profitable, just cheaper for the client.

Now, brainstorm with your clients the various products and services they are missing in their daily activities. Where can you add value? This process can be lengthy, but it's essential to make sure you don't add offerings that hurt your team, your profits, or your clients.

While you mull over adding profit centers, make sure you revisit other services you already provide that might not be profitable in the long term. Your complementary offerings should never be lower or equal in profitability with your core offerings. A safe bet for complementary offerings with high margins is information product upsells.

While we close out this chapter, here are the lessons and implementation steps Mike Bark and Chris Ragain learned when they added their respected profit centers.

Mike Bark

When Mike is launching new profit centers, he always looks for:

- An expert in that field who he knows, respects, and who could lead the new service.
- A clear understanding of expected ROI.
- If the new profit center needs financing, working with the bank to support the effort.

Mike matches client pain with colleagues who are experts in that field. He lets that colleague lead the new profit center. With this process, Mike has built an entire marketing agency within his firm. He, himself, wasn't an expert in marketing, but he found the right people to execute it so he could profit.

Chris Ragain

Chris built out an entire wealth management center for his clients. He learned that by listening to his clients daily and finding those common pains, he was well on his way to finding the right profit centers.

Chris subscribed to financial newsletters and began studying how the top analysts track and manage their portfolios. He spent years tracking their advice and subscribed to dozens of investing newsletters in order to understand patterns and common picks within the market.

What surprised Chris was that not only has he yielded above average returns, but this single profit center has now surpassed his already successful core business, both in revenue *and* profits.

That would feel great, wouldn't it?

Action Steps

1. Ask yourself, do you have your foundation in place before you take on another profit center?

2. List all of your services. What could be a complementary, new, or joint venture you could add that would be massively profitable?

3. Look deeper. Where are you missing out on upselling, downselling, and cross-selling opportunities with your new and current clients?

4. What services do you dislike that are not profitable? Consider getting rid of that service offering.

Interviews to Go Deeper

1. Add 7-Figure Wealth Management Services - with Chris Ragain (https://jetpackworkflow.com/wealth-management-for-accountants-cpa-firms-chris-ragain/)

2. How to Add Multiple Profit Centers to Your Firm - with Mike Bark (https://jetpackworkflow.com/how-to-add-multiple-profit-centers-to-your-firm-the-mike-bark-interview/)

3. Shift Your Firm to Operate in the 21st Century - with Jay Holmes (https://jetpackworkflow.com/how-to-shift-your-cpa-firm-to-operate-in-the-21st-century/)

4. Drive $100M in Non-Traditional Revenue and Services - with Edi Osborne (https://jetpackworkflow.com/drove-100m-non-traditional-revenue-services-edi-osborne-interview/)

5. Are You Missing Out on Your Most Profitable Clients? (https://jetpackworkflow.com/missing-profitable-clients/)

Recommendations

In my own business, I've had to restrain myself from going crazy and adding profit centers all over the place. This book, itself, has been on hold for a couple of years because what is most important is to ensure the first piece, your foundation, is solid before branching out.

I want you to speed ahead and add as many profit centers to your firm as possible. To get that going, I invite you to check out my company, Jetpack Workflow (https://jetpackworkflow.com/). It's one of the most advanced, but simple software applications to implement in your business to handle your workflow and processes.

Right now, you can get a free 14-day trial (https://jetpackworkflow.com/) to see if it works for your firm.

Chapter 8

Acquiring Firms to Drive Rapid Growth

Each of the chapters in this book requires some work, thought, and time. It could take months or years before seeing all the fruits of it. There's another door for growing at a much faster clip—acquisition.

You may have already received phone calls from someone offering to buy your firm. It's proven to be the fastest way to double your business literally overnight.

Now, before getting too crazy, the process of acquiring a firm can take many months. As tax season creeps in, the timeline can stretch more and more. On top of that, there may not be too many firms up for grabs. Not every small to medium size firm owner wants to sell off and retire.

On the other hand, when you can find an owner who does, that's when the fun begins.

Before you start, Wil Stunkel, Founder of Stunkel Tax & Accounting, believes, much like we've preached in this book, you must have the internal processes solidified before you can bring on any new book of business. Much like the chapters in this book describe, you can't solve your problems by throwing more clients on the fire. Your processes need to be correct, efficient, and running like clockwork.

As a disclaimer, Wil also says you need to be financially stable. There will be some legal costs of acquisitions, plus some cash out of pocket right away. Furthermore, your first few years with a new book of business might not be profitable. You'll be making payouts to the sellers for many years, plus there is normally is a turnover in clients.

The First Steps to Acquisition

What types of Firms are you interested in?

Richard Wortmann, Founder of the RW Group, built his practice around the real estate niche. As we've seen in recessions, real estate can drop rapidly. He felt uneasy. If another recession hit, he might lose a handful of clients.

Thus, in order to diversify, he acquired a complementary service: a broker-dealer. Then, he expanded into other industries. He did this by acquiring firms who had clients in more stable industries as a way to diversify his risk.

When you think about the type of firm you wish to acquire, you need to take into account:

- Its size
- The financing you can afford
- Your plan to expand with the acquired staff
- The types of clients you'll pick up
- Current economic conditions in the industry

Each Firm runs differently. If you take on the acquired staff, will your culture shift? Is the book of business in line with your vision for the future? Can you handle all the clients they have?

Richard discovered he could get better deals when he targeted firms who didn't have a succession plan in place. These firms had owners who were ready to retire, but had lost a key employee or simply never planned for the day. You can pick up great deals on firms like this.

Next, decide on financing options. For firms ready to sell faster, they might offer seller financing. For other terms, you might need to get funding from a bank to afford the large payout.

As you can imagine, this process can take many weeks of discussion, brainstorming, and narrowing down. There are many firms out there who help with acquisitions and finding good prospects. It might be worth a call to one of them to start the discussion.

Hiring a broker would, of course, come with certain fees and commissions. Getting involved in certain CPA chapters and attending conferences could be a free way to prospect for businesses looking to sell.

Here's a quick marketing tactic: you can order lists of businesses from a list broker for fairly cheap. You can test sending out a letter to various businesses who fit the criteria of size and revenue you're looking for. In the end, it may come down to getting a referral or just having your broker find the deals.

Starting the Process

You, or your broker, will make contact with the firm owner and set up a preliminary discussion. During this time, you treat it much like you are in a sales process to get a new client—you ask questions, then ask more and more.

Your first talks *are not* for disclosing any pricing or discussing terms. There's too much to do beforehand and research to explore.

Do some walking around, get a feel for the size of the team. You can ask for a prior year financial report, but you might need to sign an NDA to see them first.

At this point, you just want to gather information. Here are some things you should consider doing:

- Calculate the profit margin
- Calculate the average revenue per client
- Find out the turnover rate for clients
- Read about the staff and employee turnover
- Ask about the culture and who typically works there

It's at this point you will start getting into legal discussions. Your lawyer and his hired hands will do due diligence on the firm in order for you to come up with a fair offer. At times, this process may come after a preliminary agreement has been made. Think about the purchase agreement for your house. You've agreed to terms, but you can still back out for 30 days.

Quick tip: *Everyone looks at the revenue to formulate their asking price. On the contrary, you should be looking at the cash flow of the firm. This will tell you how a firm does each month. Are they staying afloat or sinking? It also clues you in to how fast they collect from clients.*

Making the Offer

As you pull together all the different points, your first negotiated piece will be, *"Who will finance this?"* Will the bank finance? Will it be the seller? Should the buyer pay out in cash? A major factor could also be how much cash you have available to put down.

Expect to pay out six- to seven-figures, depending on the firm, for immediate cash out of pocket.

Your lawyer and broker, based on their knowledge of the market and past experience, can give you an idea on how much to offer.

Richard Wortmann found a way to make your next acquisition have absolutely *zero* risk tied to it. For most acquisitions, you (the buyer) will make payouts to either the bank or the seller for a number of years. When Richard first made a purchase, he did the traditional route—note payable over a period of time. After three years, he maintained about 85% of the new book of business he purchased.

The problem? *The risk was all on his shoulders.*

What if all 100% of the clients walked out the door? Richard would be making payments for zero additional revenue. It would bankrupt him.

> *"It's a buyer's market"*
> —Richard Wortmann

Against common belief, you, the buyer, have the upper hand in negotiations, especially if the owner is ready for a large payout. So, Richard approached his next deal in a new way—he proposed that the seller gets payouts over five years based on the revenue from the seller's book of business.

This is a revolutionary idea.

Essentially, the seller, for five years, gets 20% of all revenue collected from clients they used to serve. This can result in larger payouts for the seller, but also puts the risk on their shoulders.

You might still have to put some money down, but you aren't buying an entire firm on the hope that all the clients don't pack up their tent. With this new strategy, the seller becomes a mouthpiece for your firm. They will do everything they can to make sure as many clients as possible stay in order to see the return later on.

Richard warns: you might not see much ROI in the first five years, but you don't put your own firm at risk. If a client leaves, you don't get paid, so the seller doesn't get paid.

Even better, as these new clients purchase more services from their new firm (aka Richard's), Richard only needs to pay out 20% for the initial services bought. He can maximize value with the new clients without giving up the profit.

Here are some other recommendations for a process like Richard's:

1. Try to acquire little to no staff. They cost too much. Also, *no partners* can transfer in.

2. Acquire as little as possible due to cost. Try to just get the book of business to avoid taxes and future costs.

Wil recommends, for more traditional purchases, to structure the payment plan for as long as you can. This way, profits aren't eaten up as you acclimate the new clients and, if applicable, team members.

Of course—make sure you get everything in writing!

Moving Forward

The first few days after acquisition can be crazy. You are getting clients up to speed and any new team members need to be brought up to speed as well. Workflow processes need to be re-examined for cracks.

It's exciting and stressful.

A good way to help ease the transition is to have, as part of the sale, 30 days for the seller's firm to introduce the clients to your firm, plus do the same for any team members. This can help with client and employee turnover.

Wil recommends essentially living inside the firm you are buying. Understand what they do differently so you can make the checklists of what needs to be changed or adapted.

You don't want the culture to shift too much. Remember, in this modern day for CPA firms, your culture can make or break team members. Don't shut them out. Many will have concerns over job security and the future of the firm. You will need to budget time for these private discussions especially with your managers and up-and-coming practitioners.

Once you go through your first acquisition, you will be able to prepare for your next one. The actual combining of firms remains the hardest part. You need the right amount of glue to keep the structure in place.

Conclusion

Acquisitions can be exciting. You read so much about them on all the big business sites. Now, you are a part of one!

It may not be newsworthy, but it's life changing for you. It's the fastest proven way to grow your business, but it's not without risk.

Your first order of business must be that everything runs smoothly at your own firm before you peek around at others. You will need a nice stockpile of cash in your account, plus the manpower to prospect for businesses near you.

Don't let the potentially long timeline for acquiring discourage you. This downtime can be when you dig into the details and look for reasons to *not* buy the firm. Play devil's advocate and figure out where this deal might not make sense.

If you can't find any red flags and the price is right, then it might be the move for you.

Think about the two ways to acquire:

- Traditional bank or seller financed options, or
- The "commission" approach where the seller gets a percentage of revenue from their old book of business.

Depending on the market climate and finding an eager seller, you could snatch up a deal this year if your firm is ready for it. Once you implement all the chapters in this book, acquisition might make the most logical sense to take your firm to eight figures and beyond.

Interviews to Go Deeper

1. Steps to Buying Another Firm - with Wil Stunkel (https://jetpackworkflow.com/buying-cpa-firm-accounting-practice-inside-interview-wil-stunkel/)

2. Grow your Firm with Acquisitions - with Richard Wortmann (https://jetpackworkflow.com/grow-your-accounting-practice-richard-wortmann/)

Conclusion

The accounting landscape continues to shift. Many firms, unfortunately, see other industries get disrupted --- whether in technology, or banking --- but never believe innovation will reach the steps of accounting firms. Firms will then sit on "auto-pilot."

We felt compelled to put this book together because of all the changes we see every day. We talk with hundreds to thousands of firm owners each year and see the trends. This book can be a help or a warning. A warning that "YOU MUST DO SOMETHING TO STAY RELEVANT."

Bookkeeping is going to the cloud. Paper is becoming paperless. Living on just referrals will slow down more and more.

We aren't "Management Consultants" or "Firm Growth Experts." We just understand the accounting industry because we live in it.

At the end of each chapter, there were special, free offers to help better your firm starting today. Don't take those offers lightly. It's our way to begin making a change in the industry, one firm at a time.

Start with just reaching out to one of us and start the conversation:

David – david@jetpackworkflow.com
Joe – joe@jccopy.com

It's 100% risk-free, no payments of any kind, just free-flowing ideas to help your firm.

It's been fun writing this for you, compiling information from the huge base of experts we've talked with. Let us know how you like it,

David Cristello
Joe Cassandra

Interview Reference

Chapter 1: Increasing Your Workflow Efficiency to Increase Capacity

1. Build a Better Workflow - with Jeff Borcshowa (https://jetpackworkflow.com/how-to-build-a-better-workflow-accounting-practice/)

2. Landing the Best Clients - with Stacy Kildal (https://jetpackworkflow.com/3-steps-to-landing-the-best-bookkeeping-clients/)

3. Ditch Timesheets and Grow Quickly - with Tim Shortsleeve (https://jetpackworkflow.com/grow-a-successful-accounting-practice/)

4. Mastering Workflow for Firms - with Damien Greathead (https://jetpackworkflow.com/mastering-workflow-for-accountants-cpa-damien-greathead-interview/)

5. Boost your Firm Profitability - with Rob Nixon (https://jetpackworkflow.com/accounting-firm-profitability-rob-nixon/)

6. Apply Lean Six Sigma to Workflow - with Dustin Hostetler (https://jetpackworkflow.com/applying-lean-six-sigma-to-your-workflow-the-dustin-hostetler/)

7. Double Revenues by Cutting 30% of Clients - with Ingrid Edstrom (https://jetpackworkflow.com/double-bookkeeping-revenue/)

8. Onboard New Clients - with Chad Davis (https://jetpackworkflow.com/how-to-onboard-new-clients-manage-a-remote-team-the-chad-davis-interview/)

Chapter 2: Making the Required Move Away from the Billable Hour

1. How to Implement Value Pricing - with Ron Baker (https://jetpackworkflow.com/how-to-implement-value-pricing-with-ron-baker/)

2. Move to Value Based Billing - with Jason Blumer (https://jetpackworkflow.com/value-based-billing-paperless-flat-cpa-firm-jason-blumer/)

3. Add 19% to Bottom Line with Value Pricing - with Steve Major (https://jetpackworkflow.com/value-pricing-adds-profit-ditch-timesheets/)

4. Price on Value and Measure Success - Kirk Bowman (https://jetpackworkflow.com/art-value-interview-kirk-bowman/)

Chapter 3: Driving Growth in Your Firm

1. Using Social Media and Other Strategies to Grow - with Jody Padar (https://jetpackworkflow.com/5-simple-steps-to-transform-into-a-radical-cpa-firm/)

2. How to Massively Profit on Your Expertise - with Seth David (https://jetpackworkflow.com/profit-on-your-expertise-seth-david/)

3. Getting Your Ideal Clients - with Nate Hagerty (https://jetpackworkflow.com/nate-hagerty-interview-get-ideal-accounting-clients/)

4. Using Content to Build Up a Client Base - with Edward Mendlowitz (https://jetpackworkflow.com/edward-mendlowitz-interview-grow-accounting-firm-manage-staff/)

5. Free Marketing Strategies for Your Firm - with Bonnie Buol Ruszczyk (https://jetpackworkflow.com/free-marketing-strategies-for-your-firm-the-bonnie-buol-ruszczyk-interview/)

6. 47 Lead Generation Tips & Tricks (https://jetpackworkflow.com/47-lead-generations-tips-accountants/)

7. The New Rules of Marketing for CPA Firms (https://jetpackworkflow.com/new-rules-marketing-accounting-professionals/)

Chapter 4: Your Sales Appointment Start to Close

1. How to Handle Objections and Close the Sale - with Martin Bissett (https://jetpackworkflow.com/top-sales-objection-close-clients/)

Chapter 5: Get Referrals and Attract the Clients You Want

1. Turn Contacts into New Clients - with David Fisher (https://jetpackworkflow.com/networking-for-accounting-clients-david-fisher/)

2. Build a Referral-Based Firm - with Michelle Long (https://jetpackworkflow.com/build-a-referral-based-cpa-firm/)

3. Working with the Best Clients Only - with Steve Pipe (https://jetpackworkflow.com/finding-freedom-firm-interview-steve-pipe/)

4. Become an Advisor for Clients - with Shelley Johnson (https://jetpackworkflow.com/become-an-advisor-clients-cpa-firm/)

5. Building a 7-Figure Firm - with Darren Root (https:// jetpackworkflow.com/building-a-7-figure-firm-the-darren-root-interview/)

6. Two Simple Techniques to get More Referrals (https:// jetpackworkflow.com/2-simple-techniques-get-referrals-accountants-bookkeepers/)

7. How to ask for a Referral from Clients (https:// jetpackworkflow.com/how-to-ask-a-client-for-referrals/)

Chapter 6: Recruiting and Retaining Top Talent

1. 3 Steps to Building an Effective Team - with Chad Ridner (https://jetpackworkflow.com/3-crucial-steps-to-building-an-effective-accounting-team/)

2. Transform Your Firm into a Profitable Powerhouse - with Paula Allgood (https://jetpackworkflow.com/transform-your-cpa-firm-into-a-profitable-powerhouse/)

3. Retain Top Talent with a Better Work/Life Balance - with Chet Buchman (https://jetpackworkflow.com/how-to-master-a-work-life-balance-program-within-your-firm/)

4. Building an All-Star Team - with Stephen King (https:// jetpackworkflow.com/building-star-team-culture-stephen-king-interview/)

5. Working with Younger Talent in the Firm - with Sandra Wiley (https://jetpackworkflow.com/how-to-build-a-team-that-fuels-firm-growth-the-sandra-wiley-interview/)

6. Empower Team to Grow the Firm - with Angie Grissom (https://jetpackworkflow.com/creating-5-star-service-scaling-excellence-angie-grissom-interview/)

Chapter 7: How to Build Out New Profit Centers

1. Add 7-Figure Wealth Management Services - with Chris Ragain (https://jetpackworkflow.com/wealth-management-for-accountants-cpa-firms-chris-ragain/)

2. How to Add Multiple Profit Centers to Your Firm - with Mike Bark (https://jetpackworkflow.com/how-to-add-multiple-profit-centers-to-your-firm-the-mike-bark-interview/)

3. Shift Your Firm to Operate in the 21st Century - with Jay Holmes (https://jetpackworkflow.com/how-to-shift-your-cpa-firm-to-operate-in-the-21st-century/)

4. Drive $100M in Non-Traditional Revenue and Services - with Edi Osborne (https://jetpackworkflow.com/drove-100m-non-traditional-revenue-services-edi-osborne-interview/)

5. Are You Missing Out on Your Most Profitable Clients? (https://jetpackworkflow.com/missing-profitable-clients/)

Chapter 8: Acquiring Firms to Drive Rapid Growth

1. Steps to Buying Another Firm - with Wil Stunkel (https://jetpackworkflow.com/buying-cpa-firm-accounting-practice-inside-interview-wil-stunkel/)

2. Grow your Firm with Acquisitions - with Richard Wortmann (https://jetpackworkflow.com/grow-your-accounting-practice-richard-wortmann/)

To watch case studies, learn more about
the software, or start a free trial, visit
JetpackWorkflow.com

Printed in Great Britain
by Amazon